For Nate and for Bob

CONTENTS

 **Jan Miller Burkins** is a full-time consultant coaching teachers, coaches, and districts toward improving the literacy learning of children. She spent six and one-half years as a full-time coach at an elementary school in Athens, Georgia, USA. She has worked as a language arts consultant for a regional educational service agency, a district-level literacy leader, a reading specialist, a literacy consultant, and an elementary classroom teacher.

In 1989, Jan received her undergraduate degree in early childhood education from Birmingham-Southern College in Birmingham, Alabama, and in 1993, earned her master's from the University of Alabama. She earned her reading specialist certification and her doctorate from the University of Kansas in 1999. Her dissertation, which was a meta-analysis of the research on phonemic awareness, was the Dissertation of the Year for the University of Kansas School of Education and one of three finalists for the International Reading Association's Dissertation of the Year. Jan is also a part-time assistant professor at the University of Georgia, where she teaches classes to students pursuing graduate degrees in literacy education. She also developed a series of courses for educators interested in becoming literacy coaches.

Jan is the author of two other books, *Coaching for Balance: How to Meet the Challenges of Literacy Coaching* and *Practical Literacy Coaching: A Collection of Tools to Support Your Work*, which includes tools contributed by practitioners from across the United States. She is also the editor of *Literacy Head* (www.literacyhead.com), a virtual magazine for creative teachers and coaches.

Jan lives with her husband, Nathaniel, and her four sons, Christopher, Duncan, Natie, and Victor.

 **Melody M. Croft** worked in public education for 30 years. She earned her bachelor's, master's, and specialist degrees from Valdosta State University in Valdosta, Georgia, USA. She began her teaching career as a second-grade classroom teacher in Tifton, Georgia. Over the next 20 years, she taught first, fourth, and fifth grades.

Melody began her work as a Reading Recovery teacher in 1994. She studied the work of Marie Clay and implemented Clay's ideas in Reading Recovery contexts for nine years. She served as her school's coordinator for Literacy Collaborative, a program based at The Ohio State University that initiates and supports school-level implementation of guided reading. When her district phased out Reading Recovery, she was the last Reading Recovery teacher standing.

Melody took her expertise in beginning reading and returned to work as a self-contained first-grade teacher for the last four years of her teaching career. She and her husband live in Athens, Georgia, where they share a home and a painting studio. She has two married children: Christian is 29 and Britanny is 25. Melody enjoys painting, gardening, and taking care of her two grandsons, Naaman and Gideon.

Author Information for Correspondence and Workshops

For consulting or workshop information, you may contact Jan at jan@janmillerburkins.com or visit her website at www.janmiller burkins.com. You may contact Melody at mmcroft@yahoo.com.

Guided reading is one of the most prevalent components of any reading program and, as we have discussed in our writing about this topic, it has a long history. Although most agree that guided reading is planned, intentional, focused instruction when the teacher helps students learn more about the reading process, misunderstandings about how to implement guided reading abound.

Herein lies the value of *Preventing Misguided Reading* by Jan Burkins and Melody Croft, nothing short of a fresh and mindful look at guided reading reminiscent of a second-generation model of guided reading that we have called for since 2001. Their explanation of guided reading encourages teachers to think about how to use it to support students in becoming strategic meaning makers rather than to serve a specific guided reading orthodoxy. Their larger aim is to clear up what they perceive to be misunderstandings of guided reading and to add to its evolving knowledge base.

Make no mistake. They accomplish their aim. They begin by offering a thorough explanation of their theoretical underpinnings and how they arrived at them as a result of their own teaching and learning. Part of this discussion centers on helping teachers see the complexities of reading. Their bottom line is that there are many tricky parts to guided reading that need to be acknowledged and addressed.

Fortunately, Burkins and Croft offer numerous ways to help teachers do just that. In this book, they list and explain 27 teaching strategies designed to show as much as tell teachers how to maximize the potential of guided reading as one part of their readers' workshop. These 27 strategies are divided among six chapters. In Chapter 1, they provide four strategies that help teachers better understand how to gradually release the responsibility of learning onto students' shoulders. Burkins and Croft make clear that the overall purpose of guided reading is to scaffold learners toward independence and that removing the scaffold when it is no longer necessary is the best way to help students become independent—rather than dependent—learners.

The intent of Chapters 2 and 3 is to help teachers rethink reading levels and text gradients. Burkins and Croft offer 10 strategies that enable this thinking to occur. Their main point here is that focusing on the many different types of readers and how to be responsive to them is centric to helping students maximize their full potential as readers.

In Chapters 4 and 5, Burkins and Croft offer numerous ideas about balanced instruction. They use eight strategies to round out their explanation, which ultimately helps teachers once again see the complexity of reading and how to address it by reconsidering what it means to be "balanced."

Assessment guides instruction, and that is exactly the point of Chapter 6, their last chapter. Here they offer five strategies, each created to help teachers better understand how they can use assessment to design thoughtful lessons geared toward using what students know to help them learn what they need to know.

All told, Jan Burkins and Melody Croft offer a valuable resource that is sure to help many teachers more fully understand guided reading by rethinking, reconsidering, and renewing their efforts to use it to help all children become proficient readers.

Michael F. Opitz
Professor of Reading Education
University of Northern Colorado
Greeley, Colorado, USA

Michael P. Ford
Professor of Reading Education
University of Wisconsin Oshkosh
Oshkosh, Wisconsin, USA

A Literacy Story: Ms. Benton Teaches Her Students to Work Through the Tricky Parts

Ms. Benton's first-grade students begin their daily literacy block with shared reading, during which the students read together a simple, patterned text that is the equivalent of a Level C reader (Fountas & Pinnell, 1996). The words of the text are written on cut-up sentence strips and then scrambled for the students to put back in order. Picture supports are drawn on the sentence strips, and students work through this exercise with increasing independence. Ms. Benton teaches strategies, such as considering print and story cues, which all the students can use regardless of their instructional reading levels.

During readers' workshop, Ms. Benton uses a cooking analogy to present a minilesson on problem-solving the tricky parts in work. After telling the story, she explains, "Today while reading and writing, you may get to a tricky part in your work. If you run into a hard part in your work today and figure it out, I want you to remember how you did it. Then, we will share our tricky parts and how we figured them out at the end of readers' workshop."

Ms. Benton then begins to pull guided reading groups, while students disperse to work on various literacy tasks. While the first group of struggling, emergent readers participates in staggered oral reading, Ms. Benton pays close attention to one particular member in the group named Liya. She has worked individually with Liya on one-to-one matching in text, and this is Liya's first day to join a guided reading group. Ms. Benton intentionally uses a text that matches the sentences the class read during shared reading. The text reads, "I have a green ball. I have a yellow crayon. I have a purple bike," and so on.

Ms. Benton observes that Liya consistently points to the words as she reads, so Ms. Benton shares this behavior with the group. She says, "I noticed that when all of you were reading, you were pointing to the words very carefully. Liya, what helped you match your pointing with your voice?"

"I just looked at the words and pointed at what I was saying," explains Liya.

At the close of readers' workshop, students share the problems they encountered during their work and the various ways they solved them. After several students, Ms. Benton can't help but grin as Liya tells her classmates, "I have been working on pointing at the words in the book and hearing what I am saying to make sure it matches. I just practiced a lot to figure it out, and today I did it just right!"

The Tricky Parts

Just as Ms. Benton's students tackled the tricky parts of their work during readers' workshop, we (authors Jan and Melody) have found ourselves over the last 20–30 years working through the tricky parts of teaching students to read. We did not even know each other over many of the years that Jan studied, practiced, and taught teachers about guided reading and Melody studied and taught students in the classroom and through Reading Recovery. We were, nevertheless, in parallel universes working through parallel tricky parts.

As we began to work together, we realized that we shared theoretical and practical perspectives around literacy learning. We both embraced guided reading and struggled with the ways the designs of various models for guided reading, or the ways we interpreted them, left us asking ourselves questions about our literacy instruction. The questions we asked of ourselves mirrored those we asked of the readers we taught: What did I try? What else can I try? Does this make sense? How do I know? Does this sound right? How do I know? Does this look right? How do I know? What can I do now?

Preventing Misguided Reading represents a synthesis of our thinking before, during, and after we heard about or implemented guided reading. This book presents our work of puzzling through the difficult parts of teaching guided reading. These challenges pushed us to reframe the ways we think about teaching reading and to act on this "revisioning" strategically. Perhaps some of these strategies will help you work through your own tricky parts as you guide groups of readers.

Why We Wrote This Book

Holdaway wrote about guided reading in 1979, and Clay wrote of it in 1991. However, it took the reading profession by storm in 1996 when Fountas and Pinnell (1996) wrote *Guided Reading: Good First Teaching for All Children*. Over the last decade, guided reading has helped us focus instruction on supporting young readers in ways that foster skill and independence. At the same time, however, misunderstandings about this method abound, and confusion in the field seems to be on the rise.

Ford and Opitz (2008b) surveyed 1,500 K–2 teachers to understand common classroom practices around guided reading. Ford and Opitz discovered much confusion in the field regarding what guided reading is and how to implement it. They suggest that "variations in understandings can often lead to significant differences in how practices get implemented" (p. 311), and their survey results indicate that this is the case with guided reading.

Meanwhile, teachers express concerns with guided reading in another venue—blogs. One kindergarten teacher writes on the website A to Z Teacher Stuff Forums, "So, I hate guided reading.... Each day I dread 10:40–11:25.... I just don't know if I'm doing something wrong or what" (DrivingPigeon, 2009). Another teacher writes on the Tales of a First Grade Classroom blog, "Guided Reading...two words I have grown to hate.... Lately I've been thinking and I've come to the conclusion that Guided Reading has become institutionalized" (DeBacco, 2008).

These frustrations are not limited to digital conversations. Melody talked to a teacher whose literacy coach comes in to observe guided reading and uses a timer and a checklist to make sure she is spending the "right" amount of time on each part of the "lesson." Jan recently talked with a literacy coach who said that her principal was campaigning against guided reading, stating emphatically that guided reading doesn't work. The principal shared an article that denounced guided reading as a failed methodology. The article was distributed by a company that sells phonics readers without illustrations, so students will learn to *really* read without relying on picture cues.

Another literacy leader expressed frustration that teachers in her building are grouping students for guided reading based solely on word recognition accuracy. Yet, another literacy coach talked about how he quit using the term *guided reading* altogether, because it means something different in every classroom.

How Did Guided Reading Become Misguided?

We see several causes associated with the confusion surrounding guided reading and discuss each in the sections that follow. The order of the causes does not imply importance or priority; rather, we connect them logically.

Lost in Translation

Historically, broad and rapid dissemination of ideas, as has been the case with guided reading, can lead to tremendous change in instructional practice. With fast and widespread change, however, come challenges. Most significantly, communication often grows congested, and misunderstandings become the unintended reality. As a result, we lose in translation the subtle or deep implications of a theory or practice.

Some argue that our most influential scholars, who by definition are the most widely read, are those most mistranslated, misunderstood, and misapplied (see Gredler & Shields, 2004). For example, in regards to writings that clarify misunderstandings of Piaget's theory, Gredler (2007) writes, "Unfortunately, these and other enlightening critiques came more than 30 years after Piaget had captivated educational theory and practice, long after the misconceptions and distortions had become institutionalized" (p. 233). These solidified misinterpretations remind us of the gossip game in which the first person tells a sentence to another person, who then repeats it to another person, and so on. In the end, the final sentence is often a laughingly unrecognizable permutation of the original.

Misinterpreted instructional methods run the risk of abandonment. Education is littered with the remains of educational trends lost in translation. Often, the reality is that we compromised the fidelity of their implementation. So, critics assemble and declare that the approach doesn't work, as researchers and publishers line up to set a new program in place. We see this trend surfacing with guided reading, and we lament the energy and resources that districts may expend in totally revamping literacy instruction that may simply need adjusting.

Unnecessary Complexity

Guided reading is a small-group model that mirrors elements of the Reading Recovery lessons. Reading Recovery and the most commonly practiced methods of guided reading are based, at least to some extent, on Clay's research on beginning reading. Reading Recovery and most guided reading models share an effort to match students to texts, the use of predictable texts to scaffold beginning readers, and a focus on understanding and teaching for reading strategies.

Reading Recovery teachers, however, participate in extensive, in-depth professional learning that is ongoing. They work with students "behind the glass," under the watchful eye of trainers and coaches, and their every instructional move is scrutinized. This effort helps Reading Recovery teachers develop skills necessary to support individually and expertly the beginning readers who struggle the most and who exhibit complex difficulties.

The difference between a Reading Recovery teacher and a classroom reading teacher is analogous to the difference between seeing a specialist and seeing a general practitioner: Both serve particular purposes. General practitioners will actually decrease effectiveness in general patient care if they focus like specialists. Similarly, classroom teachers set themselves up for frustration when they try to focus guided reading instruction as intensely as teachers of individual students, although this is part of the design of many guided reading models.

We suggest that, due to constraints on time and professional learning support, classroom teachers cannot approach reading instruction in the ways that Reading Recovery teachers do, and they do not need to. Many guided reading strategies, however, were actually developed for working with individual students rather than groups.

Instruction Driven by Commerce and the Standardization of Guided Reading

Generally, school districts do not have the time or financial resources to support teachers in ongoing professional learning in literacy. Few school districts that embark on this work with teachers are able to maintain it, as attention in districts shifts to new programs and new initiatives arise. Even teachers within schools that have literacy coaches and offer teachers consistent professional learning find themselves struggling because of the demands of the task and limitations of time.

Consequently, publishers create programs designed to standardize guided reading, which, paradoxically, is actually strongest when teachers consider the spontaneous, on-the-run learning of students. Guided reading, which generally springboards from teaching points that surface during reading, does not neatly lend itself to lesson plans that are prepackaged. Nonetheless, scripted guided reading lessons abound, and teachers, working hard to make guided reading effective with their students, are understandably inclined to rely on them.

Although programs and prewritten lessons may support teachers as they work through the tricky parts of guided reading instruction, commerce has inadvertently "institutionalized" guided reading. There is much conversation among teachers and in published texts about how to do guided reading "right."

Ironically, as we write this Preface, a book about guided reading that describes exactly what to say, when to say it, and how to implement the author's "detailed descriptions and lesson plans for all stages of reading" (Richardson, 2009, p. 5) arrived in Jan's mailbox. In many cases, guided reading has become prescriptive and regimented, even though guided reading lessons should be responsive to the needs of particular groups of readers (Fountas & Pinnell, 1996), because sound reading instruction is all about knowing how individual students interact with text (Clay, 1991, 1993, 2005a, 2005b).

External Pressures to Get Students "Reading on Grade Level"

School districts often invest in commercial guided reading products because of tremendous pressure to make sure that all of their students reach performance standards. When students fall short of these goals, even if their teachers are obviously amazing, the teachers are subject to more directives, and districts buy more programs for them to follow. Furthermore, those who create specific guided reading models want their instructional designs to hold up under the pressure of intense scrutiny and accountability. Consequently, not only do states and districts tighten classroom controls but also publishers and authors become more prescriptive.

For example, Fountas and Pinnell (1996) explain that "the purpose of guided reading is to enable children to use and develop strategies 'on the run'" (p. 2). The researchers go on to describe students in guided reading as "enjoying the story because they can understand it; it is accessible to them through their own strategies supported by the teacher's introduction" (p. 2). Finally, Fountas and Pinnell write that the point of guided reading is "for children to take on novel texts, read them at once with a minimum of support, and read many of them again and again for independence and fluency" (p. 2). In contrast, in 2009, Pinnell and Fountas defined guided reading as "small-group support and explicit teaching to help students take on more challenging texts" (p. 3). They have defined guided reading as a teacher working "with a small group of children who have similar enough needs that they can be taught together" (2009, p. 8). They go on to say, however, that the point is to provide "instruction to help the children read the text proficiently and at the same time learn more about the reading process" (p. 8).

We find the prominent roles of "explicit teaching" and "challenging texts" in this 2009 definition noteworthy in comparison to earlier references to enjoying and understanding the story with minimal support. We wonder how this change to "instruction to help," as opposed to considerations of increasing student independence, connects to the pressures under which educators presently operate.

Human Nature

Although researchers and writers offer suggestions, teachers, engrossed in work at the closest point of contact with students, usually are not conducting research or digging deeply into the results of current studies. When research reaches classrooms, it is often diluted. Yet, we tend to accept it as universal truth. We may interpret (or misinterpret) these truths through our frameworks for understanding and then apply them with strict adherence rather than flexible alignment to core principles.

When working with humans in any situation, however, no theory holds up in all contexts. Rigid adherence to any instructional principle leads to forced fits and instructional confusion. Some teachers trust their instructional reasoning and the insight of their experiences and adjust their practice to meet the needs of their classrooms. Others don't trust themselves and remain faithful to a "science" that is built on trends in human nature, travels by word of mouth, and cannot be universally applied. Opitz and Ford (2001) warn,

> We need to be cautious when an educational practice, like guided reading, begins to develop the trappings of an orthodoxy. A one-size-fits-all viewpoint begins to shape practice, and teachers find themselves struggling to make the "conventional wisdom ideal" fit their unique contexts and classrooms. (p. 1)

We interpret these overgeneralizations as natural tendencies in human nature to take an idea and turn it into too much of a good thing (Hoffman, 1998).

Some misinterpretations of guided reading practices mire intelligent and dedicated teachers in frustration and actually thwart the progress of young readers. We are concerned that this confusion will lead to a backlash in reading instruction that translates into misguided practices, such as taking all the pictures out of the books, so students will "really" read the words.

The Natural Evolution of Guided Reading

Melody returned to a first-grade classroom teaching position after working as a Reading Recovery teacher for nine years. Like many first-grade teachers of guided reading, she experienced mental and physical fatigue, because she tried to incorporate direct instruction daily into each of her four guided reading groups. She attempted to create a Reading Recovery–like format during each group. She soon realized that she could not reproduce in a small-group format the Reading Recovery lessons she had grown to understand so deeply.

In fact, as the year progressed, she concluded that she was most efficient and saw the most progress in her students when she presented new information in read-aloud and shared reading lessons and then reinforced and assessed the new learning in guided reading. She learned to limit her instruction during guided reading, using preteaching and reteaching in other instructional encounters, rather than derailing the guided reading session with the intensity of Reading Recovery lessons.

Instructional decisions such as Melody's illustrate the ways that our problem-solving around the tricky parts of guided reading actually helps us make our guided reading instruction better. In many cases, the natural evolution of ideas that guide change in literacy instruction gives us forward movement.

In terms of guided reading, we believe there is merit in adjusting some of our practices for the sake of preserving an instructional model that focuses on reading processes rather than discrete reading skills. We maintain that, if guided reading lessons today were exact replications of the original conceptualizations in New Zealand almost 30 years ago, then it would likely indicate that we as literacy educators were stagnant, rather than point to the infallibility of guided reading's original design.

Experimentation and refinement through research and practice have led to what Ford and Opitz (2008b) refer to as "second generation" (p. 310) models of guided reading. With the strategies we present here, we offer both another model for the next generation of guided reading and some instructional options for shaping your own model as you work to puzzle through the parts of guided reading that are challenging in your instructional context.

What Is Guided Reading Anyway?

Truly, there are so many permutations of guided reading that one is hard pressed to look at the variety of models dotting the educational terrain and draw consistent conclusions about what is most valuable about teaching reading to small groups of students. It is as if guided reading has become to small-group reading instruction what Kleenex is to tissues. However, by identifying the commonalities in these different interpretations and implementations of guided reading, we can at least talk about general trends in guided reading instruction (Ford & Opitz, 2008a).

Based on our study of and our experience with guided reading, we conclude that teachers of guided reading typically

- Teach lessons in small groups
- Attempt to match students to texts at their instructional reading level
- Use a text gradient of some kind to help them match texts and students
- Teach groups with a common text
- Assign students to specific groups that may change text levels but change little in terms of configuration
- Present an introduction of the text
- Listen to individual students read the text
- Scaffold student reading with prompts
- Ask students questions about the story or engage them in conversation about the text

• Engage students in some element of direct instruction based on reading behavior they exhibited during the reading

Educators tend to use the terms *guided reading* and *small-group reading* interchangeably. This works in the sense that guided reading usually *is* small-group reading instruction. Small-group reading instruction, however, is often *not* guided reading. Small-group reading instruction may also be shared reading, word work practice, read-aloud, and so forth. Throughout this book, we use *guided reading* and *small-group reading* synonymously, recognizing that the switch works well within this conversation but has limitations beyond.

It is worth noting that our understandings and definitions of guided reading are most closely aligned to those presented by Fountas and Pinnell (1996) in *Guiding Reading: Good First Teaching for All Children*. *Preventing Misguided Reading* presents the clarifications, adaptations, and supports that have helped us work through our own tricky spots as we guide student readers.

The bedrock of *Preventing Misguided Reading* is the premise that learning to read is about developing a smoothly operating reading process that efficiently integrates multiple cues and extends itself as students practice reading (Clay, 1993). Guided reading is not really about levels, benchmark texts, or offering the right prompts to students when they struggle with words. Rather, guided reading is, for us, about supporting students as they develop strategic approaches to meaning making.

Methodological Ironies

Of course, the irony of this endeavor is that we run the risk of our ideas being taken to an extreme. Calkins (2001) laments, "One of the distressing things about teaching is that in an effort to solve one problem we so often create new problems" (p. 310). When we read the works of leaders in the field of literacy instruction, they consistently tread lightly, making few (if any) absolute claims.

Calkins (2001) describes an experience she had with Donald Murray. He warned that "knowing" something is dangerous. He admonished, "Watch out lest we suffer hardening of the ideologies. Watch out lest we lose the pioneer spirit which has made this field a great one" (p. 6). Along these same lines, Miller (2002) offers this encouragement: "There are many effective ways to teach children and live our lives. No one has a patent on the truth" (pp. 6–7).

So, we neither present this information as something we *know* as absolute truth nor as a prescribed approach to literacy instruction. Rather, we present it as a collection of ideas and informed interpretations of reading research and instructional experience. These ideas have made sense in our contexts. We invite you to explore them in yours.

Assumptions of Our Readers

Our intent has been to take discussions of guided reading, which has become a widespread model for teaching students to read, to a different, sometimes more practical, level. We spend little time addressing foundational ideas related to guided reading, such as the interaction of cues in the reading process or the interpretation of running records. Rather, we assume that the reader either has an introductory grasp of these ideas or that the alternative perspectives we offer can support further exploration. So, our discussions explore, but do not depend on, instructional methodologies within guided reading as they are commonly understood and sometimes misunderstood.

Respecting the Histories of Ideas

We have worked and talked with young writers about how stories usually have a beginning, a middle, and an end, without even knowing how our work connects to Aristotle, the first to label stories with these three parts. Long before Aristotle's recording, this same concept was probably illustrated on the walls of caves. Usually, the theories we actualize in our practice grow from very deep roots. Considering an ancestry of ideas that precedes our current generation of literacy thinkers stretches our understandings of everything we do. Truly, there is little that is absolutely new, little that is original.

Opitz and Ford (2001) point out that Betts wrote about guiding readers in 1946. His work in reference to supporting readers has many similarities with later writings about guided reading. So, we water the seeds planted by Myrtle Simpson, Ruth Trevor, Don Holdaway, Marie Clay, Irene Fountas, Gay Su Pinnell, Lev Vygotsky, Jean Piaget, Emmett Betts, and many, many others. We recognize the germination of ideas and the natural growth and learning that support all thinking work. We respectfully roll our wheelbarrow of ideas along the ruts and grooves in the intellectual soil established by our literacy predecessors, some of whom are probably as far removed from us as Aristotle.

Our Theoretical Perspectives

Our philosophy of reading is rooted in an enduring respect for the complexities of the reading process as described by Clay (1979, 1991, 1993, 2005a, 2005b). We further recognize the idiosyncratic interaction of print, meaning, and structural cues, which is influenced by an array of reader factors (Rosenblatt, 2004), making each reading experience a unique interaction between the reader and the text.

In terms of learning theories, we maintain that a self-extending system is inherently constructivist (Piaget, 1967), as understandings of the reading process develop when students act on text to construct meaning (Wood, 1994). Clay (1979) describes students as enacting a "set of operations" toward the end of understanding the "precise words and meanings of the author" (p. 8). Throughout this text, we return to the idea that students learn to read with one foot in what they know and the other stepping into new understandings. This idea of dynamic support, whether from teachers or texts, is fundamentally Vygotskian (Vygotsky, 1962), and is a regular refrain throughout our descriptions of the theoretical and practical dimensions of the strategies in this collection.

Finally, although this book looks closely at some of the finer points of teaching students to read, it is rooted in the idea that teaching literacy is intrinsically political, as reading and writing are "emancipatory acts" (Christensen, 2000, p. vii). The texts we choose, the ways we define language in classrooms, and the sense of agency that we support students in developing around their learning are all elements of our embedded commitment to critical literacy that is furthered when we teach students how to read.

A Word About Collaboration

Right now, collaboration is prominent in practitioner and research literature, partially because it is such a challenge and partially because working together can lead to better student outcomes. Writing a book together is among the pinnacles in collaboration (closely behind raising children with someone or committing to a life partner). We have supported and stretched each other through this collaboration and know with certainty that this book is better because of our chemistry of ideas.

In cowriting a book, authors must negotiate the ways that their voices work together. For Jan, as a literacy coach and university instructor, her recent work has been geared toward a macrolevel of literacy instruction across a building. Among Melody's 30 years as an elementary teacher, her work as a Reading Recovery teacher for nine years and as a first-grade classroom teacher for six years has concentrated on the microlevel of teaching students to read. As much as we have been able, we have chosen to merge these respective voices in this book. Occasionally, we share experiences from one of our specific backgrounds. In these cases, we refer to ourselves in the third person.

Although Jan's slight bent is toward the theoretical and Melody's is toward the practical, we are both at home in these complementary universes. One does not coach literacy in an elementary school without a considerable amount of hands-on, up-close experience and action with students, so Jan is nimble in making the moment-to-moment decisions that make up the application of the ideas within this text. Likewise, one does not spend nine years as a Reading Recovery teacher without scrutinizing literacy on a theoretical level. Melody is well versed in literacy theory and can speak authoritatively to the understandings that support the decisions a teacher of literacy must make.

The overlap and diversity in our experiences make us particularly suited for this collaboration, and we have both been directly and deeply involved with all aspects of this text. We did not each go to our separate corners and draft our parts to cut and paste them together. Rather, we talked extensively about all aspects of the book, holding ourselves to a high standard of true collaboration. Consequently, we are equally invested in both the general and practical dimensions of this effort.

Measuring Our Words

We deliberated extensively in choosing the words that organize *Preventing Misguided Reading*. We agonized over each label in this book, arriving at final decisions that seemed certain, only to revise again and again. We both engage in constant reflection around our language and appreciate that these vocabularies serve to engage us in conversations; they are not the end of ideas, but rather the beginning. We chose the title not to criticize ourselves and others as literacy educators but to engage a sense of urgency and offer hope. Misguidance requires a shift in direction, an adjustment in thought or practice. In our misguidance, the aim of educators was honest; we just need to reflect and adjust.

We hesitantly chose the label *strategies*, because it is closely linked to Clay, whose work informs ours. The term is overused and misunderstood, however, a rather ironic twist in a book written to offer instructional clarity. Clay (1991) explains that strategies are the "in-the-head" processes that readers engage as they work to gain control while they read (p. 3). Afflerbach, Pearson, and Paris (2008) further clarify this term by pointing out that, if students are working to gain control, their use of strategies is necessarily intentional. Automatic behaviors are no longer strategies, but rather, skills. As you try some of the strategies in this book, we hope those that work for you and your students will become part of your repertoire of skills.

For us, *strategy* furthers our analogy between the ways students problem-solve in guided reading and the ways teachers problem-solve as they *teach* guided reading. Students deliberate consciously as they work in their heads, following up with changes in behavior as they use strategies in reading. Similarly, teachers can think through theoretical ideas and make strategic shifts to shape their instruction.

We talked into the wee hours of the morning, considering the nuances of miscue versus error versus mistake, processes versus systems, misunderstandings versus misconceptions, new versus assimilated, integrating versus consolidating, and on and on and on. We are "word people" who don't order french fries without scrutinizing the subtext of our language. In the end, sometimes the words we chose held up throughout the revision process, and other times labels made the cut—not because they were perfect, but because it was time to stop changing them. Our intent is always to communicate clearly and honor the expertise you bring to this book.

Organization of This Book

Preventing Misguided Reading opens with an Introduction that presents a basic orientation to a simple model of the reading process. This model undergirds all of the ideas presented in this book. After the Introduction, the volume is divided into six chapters, each one clarifying a point we consider a misunderstanding about guided reading instruction. Each chapter is preceded by a vignette that illustrates the subject of the chapter. These are nonexamples around common guided reading practices. All of the hypothetical teachers in these examples are composites of us, as we have worked through these tricky parts and engaged in these inefficient practices.

After we offer theoretical support for our clarifying idea in each chapter, we describe specific strategies for reframing your thinking or adjusting your practice. These instructional strategies are located under a common heading, "Working Through the Tricky Parts." Each chapter ends with a "Putting It All Together" section and a series of questions to support your reflection and conversation.

In Chapter 1, we take a hard look at the gradual release of responsibility (Pearson & Gallagher, 1983), maintaining that guided reading's place in this continuum of increasing student proficiency needs adjustment. We reframe guided reading's relationship to shared and independent reading. We also suggest that the role of the teacher is sometimes too prominent in guided reading, particularly in light of its positioning in the gradual release continuum.

Chapter 2 establishes a foundation for later chapters by scrutinizing the common definition of instructional reading level. We recommend that you adjust your quantitative definitions and adopt some qualitative definitions of this term. We argue that texts presently defined as instructional level may, in many cases, frustrate readers. The chapter goes on to present specific recommendations for modifying your considerations of text difficulty.

Chapter 3 takes on common assumptions about text gradients. It presents advantages and disadvantages of working with leveled texts and offers ideas for making the most of these tools. We also offer suggestions for practicing mindful language around students and text levels and for avoiding traps that lock students into narrowed identities and experiences.

In Chapter 4, we explore in depth the ways students use visual cues, or print, and the ways they use meaning and structural cues, or story. We maintain that instruction emphasizing one set of cues over another compromises students' opportunities to develop smoothly operating reading processes. The chapter includes specific strategies that you can engage to support students as they develop competency in using all of the cues a text offers.

In Chapter 5, we look at the ways students put together the cues they access during reading. We talk extensively about how to consider a student's integrated processing of cues and what an individual student's reading process says about that student's instructional needs. Then, we offer specific strategies that fit the different patterns of integrated processing common among readers.

Finally, Chapter 6 wraps up the book with a close look at the ways our formative and summative literacy assessments can inform our reading instruction. We end with assessment not because it is a last priority, but because the preceding chapters build understandings necessary for reading this chapter. Chapter 6 looks specifically at employing assessment tools to understand student reading processes. The strategies in this chapter can help you dig deeper into the stories that your literacy assessments tell you about your students.

A Few Last Words Before We Begin

We do not claim to be the last word on any idea in the area of literacy (or anything else for that matter). Rather, we simply aim to extend ideas, push thinking, and initiate conversations. We invite you to interrogate our work and extend it in ways that promote your learning to the benefit of the students with whom you work. This text is riddled with qualifying statements, such as, "We think this may be true...," "This might improve your instruction...," and "Perhaps we should look at it this way...." These phrases serve as reminders that we do not intend to offer you ideological premises to claim as absolutes, but rather we want to share some of the thinking and "fix-up" strategies that have helped us negotiate the tricky parts of guided reading.

Take our offerings into your action research and gauge which of these ideas and strategies work for you; it is up to you to determine the truth of our work in your context. We count on your scrutiny to hold us accountable, just as we rely on you to translate our ideas into your classroom practice thoughtfully.

ACKNOWLEDGMENTS

In publishing a book, one inevitably encounters tricky parts, and one's editors are the guides for navigating the bumpy terrain. We are deeply grateful for the opportunity to work with the International Reading Association in general, and Corinne Mooney and Charlene Nichols specifically. They have earned our deepest loyalty for their flexibility, their interest in helping us preserve our voice, and quite simply, their care for the project and for us. We also appreciate Tony Hart, who donned his graphic artist cape and was a hero when we all needed help materializing a vision for the cover. If you need a graphic artist rescue, you can contact him at anhart20@alumni.scad.edu.

Usually, when authors craft books, the process lasts months or years, and the writers incur debts of kindness to all those who support them along the way. *Preventing Misguided Reading* took us 50 collective years of prewriting, so there aren't enough pages to acknowledge the people who have nurtured our thinking over these many, many years of literacy work. Such a list would include everyone who has taught us and everyone we have taught.

Although imagining and shaping the ideas in *Preventing Misguided Reading* took decades of thinking and practice, we densely packed the years it took to craft this story into only a few months of writing. We wrote down all the first words over an intense two weeks and then revised periodically through equally intense weekends across several months. As we put all our energies into this demanding endeavor, our husbands without hesitation assumed the roles we stepped out of, while also making sure we were not swallowed whole by this project.

Our work consumed us like the search for alchemy consumed José Arcadio Buendia in *One Hundred Years of Solitude* (Márquez, 2006), who stopped eating and sleeping for the sake of his undertaking. And our husbands took care of us, like Rebecca, whose vigilance and care for José "kept him from being dragged off by his imagination into a state of perpetual delirium from which he would not recover" (p. 76).

If our husbands had not brought us food and made us stop writing to eat, we would now be skeletons around our keyboards, our remains among a pile of books about early literacy. If they had not forcefully taken our work from our hands and led us to places of rest or distraction, we would now be unable to form even the simplest sentences. If they had not loved us enough to say, "I will go with you to the coffee shop [or book store or library] just to be close to you while you write," we would have had less passion for our work and more emptiness now that it is done.

Although our literacy endeavors have always been supported by many, our personal lives, and the ways they fit into our professional work, have been nurtured by Bob and Nate. Thank you for working through life's tricky parts with us. We know, Nate and Bob, that you have worked as hard as we, and this book is as much yours as ours.

A Simple Model
of the Reading Process

*If fish were to become scientists, the last thing they might
discover would be water.*

S. Jay Samuels

I n this book, we offer our understandings of guided reading instruction
and work to bring clarity to some big ideas surrounding it. Our arrival
at the understandings central to this book has been comparable to fish
discoveries of water. We were metaphorically splashing around in this
work of guiding readers on a daily basis, but our shifts in understanding
came with the discovery that the reading process, rather than text levels,
is the critical part of guided reading. This idea seems obvious now. As
we will explore in this book, however, many common practices in guided
reading emphasize reading level over reading process.

Honoring the Complexities of Reading

Reading is a fantastically complicated process, the mechanisms of which
are largely invisible to an observer (Clay, 1991, 1993, 2005a). In fact,
reading is so complex that educational researchers still don't absolutely
understand how it works. There are whole books dedicated to explaining
the different models developed by reading researchers to describe how
students learn to read (Ruddell & Unrau, 2004). There exist detailed models
of the reading process that look at comprehension (Anderson, 2004;
Ruddell & Unrau, 2004; Spiro, Coulson, Feltovich, & Anderson, 2004),
others that focus on word recognition (Adams, 1990, 2004), others that
examine student attitude (Mathewson, 2004), others that consider student
interaction with text (Rosenblatt, 2004), and so on.

Because *Preventing Misguided Reading* focuses on practicality more
than theory, we present the reading process differently, attempting to label

enough of the elements we think critical without introducing a dimension of vocabulary that gets in our way. We offer a comparatively simple illustration of the reading process, recognizing its profound limitations for infinitely scrutinizing the minute details of students' reading and its tremendous utility for actually engaging in conversations about how students read. The technicality of our vocabulary inversely relates to the number of people with whom we can talk. This does not speak to the wit or wisdom of educators, but rather to the enormity of learning to read and the many subtleties that hold the potential for fine analysis and complicated study.

Simplicity allows us to broadly instruct, document, and discuss the work of readers, whereas complexity allows us to closely align our instruction to the needs of our students. If we move too far into the complexities, we run the risk of getting lost in detail, confused by semantics, or distracted by individual cases; if we step too far away from the complexity, we might allow oversimplification to push us to consider students narrowly or to generalize away from truth.

Like general practitioners and specialists, both of whom are experts in medicine, these tensions between practicality and theory, generality and specifics, are resolved "situationally." In *this* situation, we aim to bring in just enough theory to support consideration of practice.

Engaging a Vocabulary Around the Reading Process

To effectively teach guided reading, it helps to understand the reading process as it represents the ways a reader accesses and integrates information from multiple cues for the purpose of gaining understanding. This tenet is the most important idea in this book! Teaching guided reading is about teaching toward a particular student's reading process. Guided reading is not about teaching "little books." It is not about prompting for strategies or about leveling texts or students. It is first and foremost about developing in students reading processes that are efficient, or what Clay (1993) refers to as "a smoothly operating reading system" (p. 17).

Readers will access various sources of information in the process of making sense of a text. Three sources of information originally described by Clay (1979, 1991), and which educators commonly consider, are meaning (i.e., the context, including the pictures), visual (i.e., the print), and structure (i.e., the language or syntax). These three sources of information support each other, working in concert to form an interactive reading process. The redundancy of information across these cues allows readers to check themselves when they are reading by comparing what different sources of information are telling them. So, a student who reads proficiently might read a word by accessing the visual information (looking at the print) and automatically check that print information against the meaning that is already in place.

For the sake of simplicity and clarity, we chose to support the explorations in this text with a general illustration of reading that is informed by the reading process as described by Clay, but focuses our language even more. Basically, when one thinks of the pragmatics of reading instruction, there are two "biggies": Students have to read the words *and* understand them.

To represent these two dimensions, we refer to the print (e.g., letters, sounds, letter patterns, punctuation) and the story (e.g., context, language structure, pictures, vocabulary). You'll note that throughout the book, we refer to print and story in a general sense and more specifically as defined here. For example, in references like "a student who relies too heavily on print," the term *print* actually includes all visual aspects of the reading process. However, "the student studied *the* print" refers specifically to the print on the page. Similarly, when we say "the reader depends heavily on story when reading," we are referring to all the elements that offer semantic or syntactic support to the reader, such as the pictures, pattern in the text, vocabulary, and so forth. If, on the other hand, we say "the teacher read *the* story," we are simply talking about the book or story the teacher is reading and not specifically referencing the reading process. Our use of the article *the* should help you distinguish between our two uses of these terms. According to our representation, reading is the back-and-forth work of considering the print information as it supports story, and vice versa, as represented in Figure 1. This diagram illustrates the way a "good" reader engages in integrated processing of textual cues toward the end of gathering the meaning of the text.

A general way to describe the way a reader integrates these two sources of information is to refer to him or her as "balanced." The term

Figure 1. The Relationship Between Print and Story

Print   Reading   Story

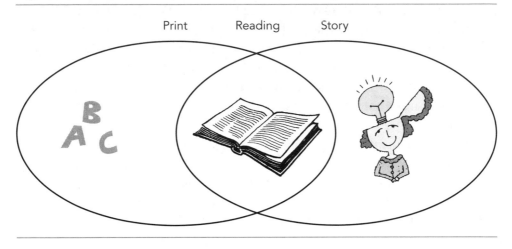

balance in the field of literacy has come under scrutiny and scholars have, with good reason, criticized it. It can represent an oversimplification of the reading process and implies that there is some moment of stasis in the act of reading. Actually, the process of reading involves constant activity and mental motion. Nevertheless, as a place to start, it is worth considering the term *balance* as a general descriptor of how efficient readers access information. By balance, we mean, are students equally proficient in drawing from print and story and, even more important, are they able to efficiently integrate this information—weighing one against the other— in ways that demonstrate a smooth reading process and support their understanding of the text?

So, in theory, a student who is engaging a balanced reading process will have comparable levels of skill in decoding words (i.e., print) and in accessing the meaning and language structure (i.e., story) of the text and will use these two information sources to check and confirm. This reading process is represented by Figure 1. When a student has a reading process such as this, he or she simply sounds like a proficient reader, making the amazingly complex text of reading appear easy.

Although a student may demonstrate a balanced reading process at a particular level of text difficulty, increasing the difficulty level of the text will betray strengths and weaknesses. As Clay (1979) suggests, "Everybody's reading behaviour can be broken down under difficulties" (p. 17).

Consider this analogy: In the day-to-day routines of life, we may feel that we can use either arm indiscriminately for basic tasks. If, however, we engage in a demanding physical task, such as push-ups, we are likely to find that one arm is actually stronger than the other. Such is the case with a reader's use of print and story. In more difficult text (i.e., frustration level), students are likely to rely on the information sources with which they are more adept. As the text increases in difficulty, this tendency to favor one system over another will cause a student to sound, or look, less and less like a good reader. Therefore, a student who does not have a balanced reading process is likely to have stronger skills in one (i.e., print or story) area or another, generally relying more heavily on one source of information and neglecting the other. For example, a student who decodes but does not comprehend well is illustrated by Figure 2.

This hypothetical student, who demonstrates a broad skill set in print and a narrow skill set in story, may engage a reading process that focuses on sounding out words or deliberating over some aspect of print. Students with this pattern in their reading may spend significant time laboring over each individual sound in the word *cat* when there is a prominent picture of a cat above the word.

Figure 2. The Reading Process for a Print-Dependent Reader

On the other hand, some students have the reverse behaviors, displaying skill and difficulty in the opposite information systems. For example, students who have extensive vocabularies, sound syntactical understandings, and a deep sense of story structure have a solid foundation in story. These students may lack, however, visual strategies or strength with print, as Figure 3 represents. These students engage a reading process that focuses on story as support for figuring out the words. They only access print in limited ways. Such readers often look at the first few letters of a word and guess without checking, or they may insert, omit, or substitute words that do not alter the text along story dimensions. Their errors often make sense and sound right, even if just to the reader.

One more model of reading is that of students who have skill in maximizing both print and story in isolation, but are not proficient at integrating the two sources of information. These students may access one source without checking it against the other. In terms of story, they may listen to books read aloud and answer questions well, and they may have extensive vocabularies. In terms of print, they generally understand how the visual system works and have some automaticity with the code. For example, they may navigate a list of high-frequency words without

Figure 3. The Reading Process for a Story-Dependent Reader

hesitation. Confirming and cross-checking print and story against each other in connected text, however, poses a challenge, so they are unlikely to self-correct their errors. These readers demonstrate in isolation skills they don't integrate in context.

In our experience, this pattern of reading behavior is pervasive. When students spend increasing amounts of time in text that is too difficult for them, they quit trying to engage a balanced reading process. For example, these students may inaccurately read in context the same high-frequency words they accurately read in isolation. Their errors are not because they do not know the words or because they do not understand the story. Their errors rise from not integrating the two. A reading process such as theirs is graphically represented in Figure 4.

Of course, we do encounter students who have limited skill sets both with print and story, as we illustrate in Figure 5. These students, in particular, drive us to distribute and integrate our instruction in print and story in thoughtful ways.

Generally, these five Venn diagrams represent the reading processes of most readers. Students' processes will vary across texts, so a student may demonstrate a balanced reading process in one text and print dependence in a more difficult text. These breaking points, or shifts in process, are

Figure 4. The Reading Process for a Student With Skill in Print and Story but Difficulty With Integrated Processing

Figure 5. The Reading Process for a Student Who Has Difficulty in Print, Story, *and* Integrated Processing

usually easy to see when students move through a series of increasingly difficult texts.

A Guided Reading Structure

In the discussions in this book, we work within a structure that generally fits the guided reading format most commonly practiced. This daily work with a new text includes a text introduction, student practice as teachers listen in, and a teaching point. However, we interpret these elements differently. For example, we suggest as a rule that teachers let students do more of the work during the orientation to the text rather than summarizing the text. Table 1 illustrates these differences.

Putting It All Together

In the face of complex models of reading, this simple paradigm of balance between print and story provides us with a vocabulary that helps us focus on and engage in dialogue around the *how* of a student's reading. Holding

Table 1. Comparison of Guided Reading Models

	Common Guided Reading Models	Our Understandings of Guided Reading
Introduction	• The teacher presents a summary of text, primes vocabulary, and sets a purpose for the reading.	• The teacher supports students in figuring out what they already know about the text. The teacher supports work with questions such as, "So what do you notice when you look through this book?" • The teacher may offer specific summary or prime vocabulary if students do not notice key elements.
Student practice	• The teacher listens to individual students read the entire text. • The teacher offers *specific* prompts that key students into the source of information to which they should attend.	• The teacher listens to individual students read the entire text. • The teacher offers *general* prompts that require students to engage in the work of problem-solving across cues. • The teacher might administer a running record.
Teaching point	• The teacher directly instructs to clarify a source of confusion in the text.	• The teacher reinforces and supports reflection around the strategies that worked as students problem-solved during the reading.
Instructional reading level	• Defined by Clay[a] as 90–94% word recognition accuracy on a running record.	• Defined by Betts[b] as 95–98% word recognition accuracy, 75% comprehension, and freedom from tension.

[a]From *The Early Detection of Reading Difficulties* (2nd ed., p. 17), by M.M. Clay, 1979, Portsmouth, NH: Heinemann. [b]From *Foundations of Reading Instruction: With Emphasis on Differentiated Guidance* (p. 449), by E.A. Betts, 1946, New York: American Book Company.

these models in your head while you teach guided reading can inform your instruction, regardless of text or level. Taking print and story even deeper and using Clay's work to look at language structure, specific print use, and meaning use on sentence and story levels will help you better understand your students as readers. We will consider these big ideas in depth throughout this book.

A Literacy Story: Ms. Hull Works Too Hard

"My guided reading groups wear me out. I can't get everything in that needs to get done!" exhales Ms. Hull as she plops down her lunch tray and herself at the table where her kindergarten team sits. The four teachers spend their lunchtime supporting each other as they talk through the challenges they face.

Ms. Hull: According to the county curriculum map, we're supposed to teach a new reading standard this week in guided reading, and my kids haven't mastered the one from last week. Are you guys having the same experience?

Ms. Sanchez: My reading groups are struggling with last week's standard, too. We can't get through a page of a book without my having to interrupt someone's reading, because they aren't one-to-one matching.

Mr. Nash: Same problem here! I feel like a prompting parrot who only knows the phrase, "Did that match? Did that match? Did that match?"

Ms. Hull: Between teaching new weekly standards, reviewing the previous ones, and constantly prompting, my guided reading stretches into the read-aloud time and then—

Ms. Sanchez: And then you don't get to it. Right there with you, except for me it's shared reading time. I have to alternate the two: one day shared reading and one day a read-aloud.

Mr. Nash: I'm doing the same thing, but it's a shame. The students really enjoy read-aloud and reading Big Books.

Ms. Hull: How in the world can we teach reading standards and a new text each day during guided reading with each small group and get everything done before lunch?

CHAPTER 1

Reframing the Gradual Release of Responsibility

"Would you tell me, please, which way I ought to go from here?"
"That depends a good deal on where you want to get to," said the Cat.
"I don't much care where—" said Alice.
"Then it doesn't matter which way you go," said the Cat.

From *Alice's Adventures in Wonderland* by Lewis Carroll

I t is hard to get lost when you have no destination. Or, perhaps, it is impossible to find your way if you don't know where you are going. Fortunately, in the classroom, we know where we want to take our students; our destination is reading independence. With clear purpose and our eyes set on a particular place of understanding, we can unfold our gradual release of responsibility map and chart a course for teaching and learning. We mark our path, stop at designated points to consider our progress, look at our map again, and reorient.

In this chapter, we challenge the idea that guided reading is a more important stop on this journey than read-aloud, shared reading, and independent reading. Because, presently, guided reading is the instructional point at which teachers are most able to address the individual needs of students, we often consider guided reading the most critical instructional context, if not the only instructional context, in a literacy framework (Ford & Opitz, 2008b). Guided reading, however, is most valuable when we strategically support it across the gradual release of responsibility.

Fundamental Ideas Behind Guided Reading

The gradual release of responsibility (Pearson & Gallagher, 1983) is a model for describing the ways that teachers decrease support for students as students begin to perform newly learned tasks independently. The model grew from Vygotskian (1962) principles that emphasize the use of scaffolding or "collaborative dialogue" between more capable others and the learner. This dialogue becomes the vehicle for observable shifts in student learning. Vygotsky's zone of proximal development is the space between the student's present capabilities and the "more knowledgeable other's" desired goal for the student.

The term *scaffolding the learner* has become synonymous with guided reading. The phrase brings to mind a physical construction that supports students as they engage in the work necessary for becoming literate. Historically, the teacher serves as the scaffold, which means that the teacher offers more support or does more of the work when the task is more difficult for the learner. For example, in guided reading, the teacher will introduce the text, whereas in independent reading, students will orient themselves to the text. This variation works theoretically, because the difficulty of the text changes from guided to independent reading. Where the text is harder, the teacher does more of the work.

We suggest, however, that if we teach students to let the text support them, we foster more independence in students. In order to do this, we can teach students to rely on the text rather than on the teacher for scaffolding. This does not mean that a teacher does not support students; it means that we support them in learning to support themselves, and we do this systematically across instructional contexts. In isolation, guided reading has limitations. It can be powerful, however, when it is incorporated within a complete literacy framework that allows for an authentic, gradual release of responsibility.

Clay (1991) describes in detail a daily literacy framework, which includes read-aloud, shared reading, guided reading, and independent reading. She explores each one and examines the relationships between them. She explains that the teachers with whom she worked discovered that they could use the same book with students at different points along the gradual release of responsibility. The teacher simply works differently with students in each of the instructional contexts. The following paragraphs explore this idea.

Read-Aloud

At this point in the framework, students rely on peers and adults to show them how reading works. Clay (1991) describes the power of reading to students,

> When a story is read...the shape of the story is created, the characters emerge, and the style of discourse and the literary turn of phrase are "heard"...new language forms are introduced to the ear,...and meanings can be negotiated in discussion before, during, and after the story reading. (p. 171)

Teachers model reading for students during read-aloud, a critical component in reading instruction, as it gives students access to sophisticated text without the limitations print places on them. A read-aloud program (we use the word *program* to refer to the big picture of the combined read-alouds that fit together as a thoughtful plan for instruction, not a commercial program) may involve think-aloud or interactive components and focus heavily on the meaning "within the text," "about the text," and "beyond the text" (Fountas & Pinnell, 2006, p. 33). This phase of reading instruction within a systematic instructional structure is necessarily story heavy, since the students are not looking at copies of the text but are simply listening and rely on meaning and structural elements to help them comprehend.

In the simplicity of the daily read-aloud resides a powerful tool that defines and depicts the role of the reader and the act of reading. The students listen, respond, and question throughout the text, while making connections that inform their individual reading processes. The connections students make between read-aloud and guided or independent reading range from very simple to advanced, depending on where the students are working along their own learning continuums.

Students often incorporate some aspect of the reading process during guided reading, because they observe their teacher demonstrate that aspect during read-aloud. For example, some students monitor their reading, because they witnessed their teacher stop reading and say, "Oops! That didn't sound right. I better go back and read that again." Other students may reread during guided reading when something doesn't make sense, search a text for confirmation of a prediction, or make connections between the pictures and the visual cues. Students are more likely to use strategies if they observe their teacher demonstrating during read-aloud (and think-aloud). So, read-aloud, as part of the gradual release of responsibility, feeds naturally into the work of guided reading.

Because elementary teachers are skilled in reading aloud to students in ways that engage and entertain them, thoughtful planning for read-aloud is often the first piece to go when the planning schedule gets tight. This effort to save time may actually perpetuate a false economy in classrooms. To engage students in exploring the deep understandings of a text requires that even the most experienced teacher plan carefully. Claudia Taxel, a colleague who has been an elementary literacy coach for eight years, calls the systematic attention to the deepest themes of a text "mining the book." Although read-aloud is not the focus of this text, we felt that, as part of the gradual release of responsibility, it deserves prominence in a complete reading framework because of the ways it can support students' deep comprehension during guided reading. Students' movement from read-aloud to shared reading is, in a Vygotskian sense, about transitioning from "other-regulation" to "self-regulation."

Shared Reading

Next in the gradual release of responsibility, the students begin to assume some responsibility for the reading work as they participate in shared reading. Holdaway created shared reading in 1972 in an effort to mimic in classrooms the intimacy of the bedtime stories that some students enjoy at home. The idea behind shared reading is that, unlike read-aloud during which students are only listening to the story, the teacher uses a Big Book or an enlarged version of some text to give all of the students access to the print. During shared reading, teachers scaffold students by explicitly teaching them how to strategically use the text to support reading. The teacher makes transparent his or her thought processes while demonstrating the ways strategic readers let the text scaffold their integration of print and story.

Shared reading is necessarily instructionally dense, as the learning during shared reading will next move into guided reading. Teachers use this time to give students valuable practice with their complete reading processes. Direct instruction finds a logical home in shared reading, offering us opportunities to teach toward understanding the reading process. Whereas the guided reading context is a session, the shared reading context is truly a lesson. These lessons may stem from behaviors that teachers observe during guided reading sessions. Ideally, shared reading lessons teach elements of the reading process, but bend to demonstrate how the parts of the entire process interact. Even though we may focus on a particular print or story element during a shared reading lesson, we always try to put the pieces back into a cohesive whole.

The accountability pressures of the instructional day can distract us from our goal of teaching toward the reading process. Although it is worthwhile to stop and ask one student to explain how he knew a word and then ask another student why she self-corrected a particular sentence, it is valuable to reconnect these detours with the whole act of reading. We want students to understand from the very first day of shared reading that the act of reading is story driven or, more simply, an act of discovering what the author is telling us. We want students to engage in mindful reading (Mooney, 1990), even if the shared reading lesson sometimes involves focused attention on some subcomponent of the reading process. Table 2 illustrates language from shared reading lessons that supports the entire reading process.

Table 2. Language From Shared Reading Lessons

Language Focused on Details	Language Focused on the Reading Process
"Count how many periods are on this page."	"Follow along as I read this page and listen to what my voice does when I get to a period." "Now, let's read this page together and...."
"What part of speech is this word?"	"Listen to this sentence. What nouns can you find that are both in the words and in the pictures? Now, let's read the whole sentence together."
"On this page, find a word that rhymes with *dog*."	"Today during shared reading, I want you to think about rhyming words. Whenever you hear or see a rhyme in the story, give me a thumbs-up." "How does the rhyme in this story help you figure out this tricky word?"
"Characters are the people or animals doing the action in the story. Name the characters in this story."	"The main character is always the person or animal that the story is mostly about. I need someone to point to a sentence in the story that shows us something about the main character so that we can read that sentence together and think about what the author wants us to know about that character."

Table 2 also illustrates how to explore topics related to the details of text within the context of related reading. This section does not imply, however, that one should never consider elements of print in isolation. Sometimes it is most efficient to say in shared reading, "How many periods (verbs, nouns, rhyming words, etc.) are on this page?" Because you have the benefit of an entire text that everyone can see, however, shared reading can involve considering how the details inform larger understandings. Attention to a reading skill, such as predicting or noticing punctuation, can begin and end with considerations of the whole puzzle by asking students to read or reread a passage without interruption as they think about story. Students, according to Mooney (1990), can focus on print details or conventions in relationship to the context of the whole story in order to solve problems they encounter in the text.

Students learning along a continuum in which they assume more and more responsibility can carry what they learn in shared reading's large-group context into their individual practice within a guided reading lesson. Thus, students learn and practice strategies in shared reading that they will apply with near independence during guided reading.

Guided Reading

The direct teaching of skills and strategies should largely occur outside guided reading. Attention to details or individual cues should be limited and, according to Clay (1991), "these are only brief detours and students quickly return to reading the text *mostly by themselves* [italics added]" (p. 199). Guided reading is an indispensable arena for linking skills and strategies that you have already taught, modeled, and practiced together during read-aloud, shared reading, and even individual conferences.

Within the larger context of a literacy framework, teachers scaffold reading behaviors by modeling them through read-aloud and engaging in reading with students in shared experiences. Rasinski (2003) explains that the continuum begins with modeling and ends with independence, and the "gulf" in between the two is where "scaffolding happens" (pp. 56–57), rather than during the guided reading session. Thus, the strategy or reading behavior that students practice in guided reading is not novel, but the teacher introduces and exercises it through varying levels of support until the practice reaches guided reading, one level removed from independent reading.

In guided reading, it is the student's job to connect across the text, mobilize already learned reading behaviors, and engage in the heavy work of integrating cues from multiple sources of information. With near independence, the student engages the strategies explicitly introduced during shared reading. At this point in the release of responsibility, the teacher mostly observes the students, before completely releasing them to independence.

During guided reading, teachers can ask themselves, can my students do it without persistent prompting from me? Through observation, which is the primary teacher role in guided reading, teachers determine what they need to revisit with their modeled (i.e., read-aloud) and interactive (i.e., shared reading) lessons.

Independent Reading

As the last point in a gradual release of responsibility, the reading behaviors students now have in place automatically mirror those practiced and solidified in shared and guided reading. There is little difference in the how of students' reading as we look across shared, guided, and independent contexts. The reading process remains the same in all of the instructional formats. The texts and the varying support of the teacher serve to facilitate this consistency.

Presently, it is not uncommon for students to practice a fractured reading process during guided reading, because teachers sometimes assume that, once the student returns to easier text, the student will smoothly integrate sources of information. With this paradigm, students rarely have the opportunity to engage a balanced process under the watchful eye of the teacher. We suggest, however, that the way readers sound in guided reading is likely to be the way they will sound when they read independently. If they don't put all the pieces together with you, they are unlikely to do so when they read alone. Furthermore, the more they practice a reading process that is not smooth in guided reading, the more likely they will habituate this inefficient process and carry it to their independent practice, making it very difficult to change later.

Rather than students practicing different reading processes in shared, guided, and independent reading (i.e., practicing the parts in guided reading and presumably putting them together in independent reading), teachers can truly capitalize on the ways the gradual release of responsibility helps students learn and practice efficient interactions with text. If students are working with text differently across the gradual release, then we are missing the reinforcement inherent in the gradual release model and may take fragmented versions of the reading process from guided reading into independence.

Teachers can scaffold students up to this point of independence, but not by breaking a process into its parts along the way (Tharp & Gallimore, 1988). Rather, simplifying the work through scaffolding means that the complete task, in this case integrating information from cues for purposes of attaining meaning, is practiced in all stages that lead to this point of independence. Eventually, students read independently, exercising a self-extending reading process, because this complete reading process has been at the heart of all of the points of learning along a continuum of gradually assuming responsibility. Hence, scaffolding toward independence is not about teachers knowing how to hold the readers up; it is about knowing how to let the readers go.

Table 3 illustrates the gradual release of responsibility as it is sometimes inconsistent. In contrast, Table 3 also presents consistency of language and reading process across the gradual release of responsibility. As the table illustrates, if we want students to develop and habituate a smoothly integrated reading process, working efficiently with print and story and the interplay between them, then we need to give students the opportunity to work through this process in each stage of the gradual release of responsibility.

Working Through the Tricky Parts of Guided Reading

Strategy #1: Connect Literacy Instruction Across Instructional Contexts

As we have discussed in this chapter, we believe that connecting instruction across modeled, shared, guided, and independent reading allows teachers to gradually shift to the students the responsibility for the literacy work. Although many recognize the heavier responsibility of teachers in read-aloud versus guided reading, we can work even more systematically by thoughtfully moving an element of literacy work along the gradual release continuum.

Table 3. Consistency of the Reading Process Through the Stages of the Gradual Release Process

Stage	Inconsistency	Consistency
Read-aloud	Teacher reads aloud *without* thinking aloud about problem-solving.	Teacher reads aloud and *occasionally* references the ways that print and story work together to aid problem-solving.
Shared reading	Structured lesson focuses heavily on details or attends to too many different points.	Structured lesson *explicitly* teaches and models the ways print and story work together to aid problem-solving.
Guided reading	Teacher-directed *lesson* carries students through text that is too difficult for students to integrate print and story without relying heavily on the teacher to prompt or redirect. The story is fragmented and the students cannot integrate cues efficiently.	Teacher-facilitated *session* in which students *actively* integrate print and story to problem-solve under the watchful eye of the teacher who documents, supports as necessary, and looks for quick teaching points to reinforce during guided reading and other teaching points to take back and address explicitly during shared reading.
Independent reading	Students read independently, practicing a fragmented reading process they habituated during shared and guided reading in texts that were too difficult or that teachers used to focus student attention on subskills.	Students read independently, engaging a balanced, integrated, self-extending reading process. They *independently* access print and story to solve problems as they read for meaning.

Consider the following classroom scenario that illustrates the connectedness between read-aloud, shared reading, guided reading, and independent reading:

Ms. Allen, a first-grade teacher, *reads aloud* to her students daily and is systematic in teaching them to consider the larger themes, or big ideas, of stories. Their read-aloud lesson helps students understand that writers communicate with readers and that reading is a meaning-making endeavor. Ms. Allen thoughtfully teaches her students to notice subtleties in the text and supports deep discussion about big ideas. Students take with them this orientation toward meaning when they encounter a text during shared reading.

With *shared reading*, students have constant access to the pictures and can use the shared print to make connections as they integrate cues. Ms. Allen continuously teaches and supports the students' active efforts to examine one source of information against another. She is strategic about helping them attend to the details of a particular source of information, but she is systematic about bringing this focus on detail back around to integrating cues and reading for meaning.

On this particular day, Ms. Allen is teaching students to look at the first letter of the word, let the picture help them predict based on the initial print cue, return to the print to verify by looking at the entire word, and then reread to refocus on meaning. This process of integrating cues is one Ms. Allen has, and will continue to, modeled and practiced with her students in shared reading contexts. The students are learning about integrating and cross-checking as they work through Big Books and stories projected on a screen with a document camera. Ms. Allen continuously reinforces a focus on thinking deeply about the meaning of the story. She has been excited lately as more and more of her students are becoming efficient in monitoring and self-correcting their reading during guided reading.

Ms. Allen judiciously prompts during *guided reading*, because she knows that every time she gives students a specific prompt, they rely on her rather than stepping into independence. During guided reading, Ms. Allen says things like, "You know how to figure that out. I have seen you do it during shared reading" and "What can you try?"

Ms. Allen observes Joe engage a strategy that she has been teaching during shared reading. After everyone has read the text, Ms. Allen asks Joe to explain how he figured out the tricky part of the story. She reiterates his explanation, reinforcing for the other members of the group the process she taught earlier.

Ms. Allen says to Joe, "Wow! The reading work you did solved your problem." Then, to the class, she says, "When he got stuck on a word today, Joe did exactly what we practiced in shared reading. I watched him look at the letters and search the picture and come up with a word. Then, and this was really something, he went back to the letters and looked at the whole word. I didn't even remind him to check. After that, he remembered to reread the whole sentence again and think about the story. He just remembered from shared reading."

While they are reading, Ms. Allen listens to each student and makes anecdotal notes and running records. She takes care in selecting accessible texts for her guided reading sessions, giving the students material in which they can actualize an integrated reading process. She knows that this practice during guided reading will carry over into their interactions with text during independent reading.

After practicing a smoothly operating reading process in shared and guided contexts, students often have efficient, established strategies for processing text. Ms. Allen listens to her students *read independently* during readers' workshop and is pleased to see that many are beginning to demonstrate automaticity with procedures she carefully supported through the gradual release of responsibility.

We can capitalize on the gradual release of responsibility by focusing our instruction consistently across instructional contexts. We support students when we carry an instructional focus through work that moves from teacher direction to teacher support, and finally to student ownership.

If we change the demands of the task, students practice one process in shared reading, another in guided reading, and still another in independent reading. This instructional potpourri would be a bit like Jan's son's cello teacher modeling and thinking aloud about how to hold the bow, engaging Christopher in shared work on his posture, supporting him in a guided context as he tries to hear whether a note is in tune, and then releasing him to independently put all these together and practice playing the cello. Such instruction is likely to actually compromise Christopher's cello playing process and leave him confused as well about each of the individual subskills of holding the bow, working on his posture, and playing in tune. Rather than a gradual release of responsibility, this would be an *abrupt* release of responsibility!

Instead, we can work backward through the release continuum, first considering what we want to see students demonstrate independently. Then, we can look for this intact demonstration of control within the guided reading context. Where it is lacking, we can teach directly during shared and even modeled reading.

Strategy #2: Describe Guided Reading as a Session Rather Than a Lesson

When you look up *lesson* in the dictionary, you find words such as *lecture*, *seminar*, and *tutorial*. These words, including *lesson*, convey a heavy teacher presence in work that gives students fewer opportunities to develop independence. With a lesson structure, there are implications of detailed planning and teacher implementation.

The planning of guided reading rests heavily, but not exclusively, in text selection and teacher intention in setting students up for success as they practice an intact reading process. Informed text selection facilitates guided reading encounters that are more session-like than lesson-like. This means that guided reading sessions are predominantly time for students to practice. Clay (1991) explains that guided reading includes teacher support with focusing, problem-solving, connecting, and discovering. She continues, however, by stating that "these are only brief detours and students quickly return to the main task of reading the text *mostly by themselves* [italics added]" (p. 199).

In contrast, the words *conference*, *assembly*, and *gathering* are thesaurus offerings for *session*. We do not suggest that teachers refrain from guiding during guided reading. We do suggest, however, that guidance differs from tutoring or direct instruction. The term *session* carries with it connotations of cooperation and spontaneity that can be lost in the structure of a lesson. For example, textbooks and professional literature that offer preplanned, guided reading lessons often contradict the essence of guided reading. Table 4 contrasts our ideas around this language of guided reading.

This seemingly minor adjustment in language from lesson to session is a precursor to shifting your thinking, and subsequently changing the ways we interact with students during guided reading.

Strategy #3: Establish Routines That Require Students to Assume Control

Teachers know that simple procedures, like having the students handle the book rather than the teacher turning the pages for them, require students to do the work of interacting with the text. We suggest that you look for places in your instructional practices where you can establish routines

Table 4. Contrasting Guided Reading Terminology

Guided Reading Lessons	Guided Reading Sessions
The teacher directs the work.	The teacher facilitates the work and engages students in assuming responsibility.
The preplanned instruction is delivered regardless of student need or inquiry relative to the reading of the text.	The teacher is responsive to the needs of the students within the particular session.
The lesson is mostly direct instruction.	The session is mostly in a conversational format.
The teacher talks a lot.	Students read a lot.

that require students to do the heavy lifting of text processing during guided reading.

One of the most valuable ways to turn the responsibility for the work over to the students early in the guided reading session is by introducing the text in ways that are broad. For example, rather than saying, "This book is about a little dog who gets lost," you might say, "Look through this book and see what you notice about the story." As you listen to students' descriptions and contributions, you can observe whether they leave out key elements that are critical for their understanding. Offering only the necessary elements of a specific introduction *after* the students explore the text on their own teaches them what to do when they come to a book, encourages independence in reading, and gives teachers a window into students' background knowledge. This work is inherently differentiated.

For example, you might ask students to give you a thumbs-up when they solve a problem and check their solution against another source of information. This nonverbal cue is engaging and simple and reminds students to work through the text thoughtfully. A thumbs-up after problem-solving does not interrupt reading that has already been interrupted by a problem. It also helps teachers watch to make sure students reread for meaning.

Another example of giving students responsibility for their work is having them turn to partners at the guided reading table and retell the story to each other. If students know they will have to recast the story in this way, they will read with particular attention to meaning. All of the work remains on the shoulders of the student, and teachers can listen to the retellings to confirm understanding, look for teaching points, and identify strategies to revisit in read-aloud, shared reading, or individual conferences. Following is a vignette that illustrates how a teacher shifted responsibility to students for thinking about the story:

First-grade teacher Ms. Jai asks her literacy coach, José, for help. "Every day I begin every guided reading lesson the same way. The students know to expect a new book to appear with a brief introduction. For instance, today in one group, I held up the front of the book and said, 'The title of today's new book is *The Little Red Hen*. In this book, a little hen asks for help in making some delicious bread, but no one will help her, and so the poor hen has to do everything herself.' And then, just as you have taught me, José, I asked a question to engage the students. I asked, 'Have any of you ever needed help doing something?'" Ms. Jai knows that this question invites the students to converse about their experiences and thus lay a foundation for later connections to the text as they preview the illustrations and begin reading.

Ms. Jai continues, "After a few minutes of conversation, I said, 'Look at the pictures now and see what the hen needs help with and who won't help her. As always, the students flipped through the pages, glanced at the pictures, and closed the book and declared, 'I'm done!' They turned those pages so fast," Ms. Jai declares in frustration, "that I had to fix my hair from the wind! When I repeated the question, they could neither tell me what the hen needed help with nor who wouldn't help her, even though these are clearly represented in the pictures.

"I have taught my students the importance of previewing the pictures by modeling in read-aloud, looking carefully at the pictures together during shared reading, and prompting them to use the pictures during guided reading, but it's always the same thing: a wind storm as they flip through the pages! Then I have to go back and prompt them more specifically, asking questions directly related to the story, like 'Who is that sitting on the couch while the Hen is working? Why?' How do I get them to look carefully at the pictures independent of my prompting?"

José helps Ms. Jai reflect and understand that, by adjusting her prompts to support her students when they didn't use strategies on their own, she was actually enabling their inaction. José helps Ms. Jai develop a plan for adjusting her instruction throughout her literacy framework. Over the next week, she tries his recommendations, integrating them into all of the instructional contexts of the gradual release of responsibility.

During read-aloud, she says to the class, "Today I am going to read *Goldilocks and the Three Bears.* But before I read, I'm going to look at the pictures on each page. I'm going to ask myself this question, what's happening?" And so, Ms. Jai proceeds on every page to ask the question, look at the picture, and then describe the action. After a few pictures, the students begin to offer their opinions of what's happening in the illustrations.

During shared reading, Ms. Jai shifts more of the responsibility to the students by letting their investigations of the illustrations serve as the introduction of the story. When she facilitates a picture walk prior to reading a Big Book with the students, she has them say aloud together, "What's happening?" She gives them a few seconds to look at the picture, then she calls on a few students to describe their thinking. Eventually, she prompts less and simply says, "Let's look at the next picture. What question are you asking?" The careful observations of the students form a generous introduction to the text, and the students are ready to read, even though Ms. Jai has not explicitly introduced the book.

Ms. Jai has primed her students well for the picture walk in the new text for guided reading. As she had done in shared reading, Ms. Jai reinforces the independence of her students as they dive into the work of figuring out what the story is about. Instead of offering the students an introduction to the book, she asks, "What is this story about?" As the students turn from the title page to the first page of the story, she asks, "How many of you asked yourself, what's happening? when you looked at the picture?" She holds accountable those who claim to have engaged the strategy by asking, "What did you find out?" She celebrates their independence and their thinking, which encourages other students to look closely at the illustrations and figure out what the story is about.

In this vignette, Ms. Jai accomplishes several objectives. First, by capitalizing on the gradual release of responsibility, she increases students' focused attention to the meaning of the texts, establishing behaviors for deep processing that they are likely to habituate during independent reading. Second, she assesses student application of the strategy and can reinforce it during shared reading. Finally, she intentionally removes herself from a role of responsibility, placing the work of guided reading squarely on the shoulders of the students.

As Ms. Jai experienced, excessively prompting students can develop habits of dependency. Furthermore, prompting frequently becomes a habituated teacher behavior. Setting in place specific routines for breaking habits helps teachers *and* students step into roles more appropriate to guided reading. Similarly, if we tell students what a story is about in guided reading, how do they develop habits of figuring out what a story is about when they are reading independently? Knowing how to figure out what the story is about and knowing how to access the pictures to support comprehension are important strategies to support systematically during guided reading, so students can engage them in the exact same ways as they read independently.

Strategy #4: Teach Students in Guided Reading Groups Only When It Meets Individual Needs

Most who implement guided reading adhere to the idea that every student needs to be in a guided reading group. We think, however, that guided reading is most appropriate for helping students establish self-extending reading systems and for practicing and extending strategies learned in other instructional contexts.

There is preliminary work in which teachers must engage some students. For example, students who do not know how to match their voices to the text in a one-to-one fashion may learn this most efficiently in a shared reading context in small-group or whole-group formats. For these students, guided reading is often an inefficient methodology for extending their emergent literacy behaviors. So, if students are not yet demonstrating processes inherent in reading, you may wait to teach them in guided reading. This does not mean that students have to know all their letters (or all of any set of discrete pieces of information) before they begin guided reading. It does mean that if students don't know how to hold a book, they may learn this better individually or in shared reading contexts.

Similarly, students who are growing rapidly along a learning continuum, because they are engaging a balanced, smoothly operating, self-extending reading process as they move along a text gradient, do not necessarily have to work in guided reading groups. If you conference with individual students who are already proficient and engage them in massive independent practice in increasingly difficult text, with which they are highly successful in each successive level of difficulty, you may support their growth more efficiently than by forcing them to work within a level that allows you to accommodate a group. You can appropriately support their extensions into more difficult text by engaging them in small-group shared readings that stretch their print and story skills, in literature circles and book clubs that read about common topics rather than on common levels, and by individually monitoring the volume and quality of their independent reading.

Not all students always need to participate in a guided reading group in the traditional sense. For example, the CAFE model (Boushey & Moser, 2009) for structuring literacy work is one design that tightly aligns instruction across the literacy framework and offers flexible deviations from the rather entrenched idea that everyone always participates in guided reading. Some students may participate in "guided reading" groups that are actually shared reading opportunities. Others may benefit from guided reading groups that you build around reading processes rather than levels. Still others, because their learning precedes or moves beyond the reading work traditionally supported along the gradual release continuum in a particular group, may benefit most from individual conferences.

Putting It All Together

The literacy framework that commonly guides instruction is embedded in a model of gradually releasing responsibility to students. We scaffold students across this continuum, but scaffolding has evolved into helping, which we sometimes offer through extensive and specific prompting. We can instead engage read-aloud, shared reading, guided reading, and independent reading to systematically scaffold students as they learn how to help themselves. In addition, we can fine-tune our prompting so that more of the problem-solving responsibility in guided reading rests with the students.

Furthermore, not every student will benefit from guided reading all the time, and it is appropriate to use our professional judgment to flexibly consider and reconsider whether guided reading in groups is meeting the current needs of individual readers. Adherence to a guided reading model in which every student participates in guided reading daily may limit the progress of our students and frustrate us. Rethinking our guided reading structures within the gradual release of responsibility can give us more flexibility, more success, and less frustration. Certainly, we can offer students different routes as they journey toward becoming literate.

QUESTIONS FOR REFLECTION AND CONVERSATION

1. At what points in the literacy framework are you explicitly teaching strategies? How is this strategy instruction supporting or hindering student independence? How do you know?

2. How does the growth of individuals in your classroom relate to the work you are doing in guided reading? Which students in your classroom might benefit from alternatives to or variations on guided reading? Why?

3. Who is working harder in guided reading—you or your students? How do you know?

4. For what work in the reading framework have your students taken responsibility? How do you know?

5. What does releasing students to independence look like in your classroom? Is this working? Why or why not?

6. With what in this chapter do you agree? Why? With what do you disagree? Why?

A Literacy Story: Mr. Stevenson Groups His Students for Guided Reading

Mr. Stevenson, a second-grade teacher, invites his literacy coach to observe his four reading groups and give him an outside perspective on whether the texts are appropriate.

Mr. Stevenson believes that his students are appropriately placed in groups; they all scored between 90% and 94% on word recognition in a benchmark book on the levels in which they are currently grouped for instruction. The students also passed the comprehension portions of the benchmarks, even though they consistently missed the questions that required them to make inferences or apply higher order thinking skills.

The literacy coach observes Mr. Stevenson and the students during guided reading over the course of a week and learns that the group in Level P does not consistently make inferences critical to understanding the text, and they usually don't notice when their reading doesn't make sense. The group working from Level M texts seems to be in appropriate texts that they manage with solid comprehension and an integrated, fluent reading process with little or no help from Mr. Stevenson.

The groups in Levels J and K, however, have significant issues managing the print demands of the text. When Mr. Stevenson prompts them specifically to try a series of strategies, they are able to figure out many of the words. Their work with print, however, interrupts their attention to story. Although they know generally what is happening in the story, there is occasional confusion that they leave unresolved unless Mr. Stevenson notices it, draws their attention to it, and helps them clarify.

The next day, when the literacy coach administers a set of running records, the readers working in texts at Levels J and K all score between 89% and 91% on word recognition. These numbers confirm for Mr. Stevenson that the students are in appropriate books. He explains that he feels that the difficulty of the text offers them the challenge they need to progress. His literacy coach, however, believes that the opposite is happening and that the struggles in which the students have to engage actually impede their progress.

CHAPTER 2

Revisiting Instructional Reading Level

*To dig for treasures shows not only impatience and greed,
but lack of faith.*

From *Gift From the Sea* by Anne Morrow Lindbergh

Some treasures are a matter of timing, others chemistry, and still others magic. Learning to read is a little of all three. But timing requires of us patience, chemistry requires experimentation, and magic, of course, requires faith. And when we dig for treasures, they can become contrived. In *Charlotte's Web* (White, 1999), the minister explains that "the words on the spider's web proved that human beings must always be on the watch for the coming of wonders" (p. 85). These wonders happen daily in guided reading groups when students read from texts in which they can extend their own learning. But we find ourselves working for "wonders," or digging for "treasures," when students are in texts that are too difficult for them. Their success rests on our support, or our effort, rather than their independence.

Over 60 years ago, Betts (1946) coined the term *instructional reading level*. He first wrote of the appropriateness of text in his 1946 book *Foundations of Reading Instruction: With Emphasis on Differentiated Guidance*. He described instructional reading level as follows:

> There should be no strain or fatigue at the instructional level. Criteria for evaluating reading performance at the instructional level include: I. a minimal comprehension score seventy-five percent, based on both factual and inferential questions, II. Accurate pronunciation of ninety-five percent of the running words, III. Ability to anticipate meaning, IV. Freedom from tension in the reading situation. (p. 449)

This definition of instructional reading level differs from the one most teachers utilize in guided reading today. Most prominently, the instructional shift from Betts's 95–98% word recognition accuracy to what is now the norm of 90–95% accuracy has introduced a level of text difficulty that we believe leads to inauthentic estimations of text appropriateness and seriously interferes with the progress of many students.

Allington (2006) reviewed research related to text appropriateness and student learning and found that the level of difficulty inversely relates to the learning. He further states that "many, many students are confronted daily by texts that are too complex for optimal learning" (p. 60). In contrast, many educators believe that, in instructional-level texts, "the difficulty of the text and tasks needs to be beyond the level at which the student is already capable of independent functioning" (Tyner, 2004, p. 32). We maintain that the work of guided reading needs to be mostly a habituation of the known, as the next stage in the gradual release is independence. If guided reading is beyond student skill levels, how then can they take these skills into independence?

This idea that guided reading text needs to be hard is often coupled with a contradictory philosophy: "Reading at the instructional level also allows students to build the use of effective cueing systems" (Tyner, 2004, p. 32). Reading difficult text, however, diminishes the orchestration of print and story, because the relatively independent functioning of the reader breaks down, hampering student opportunities to "build the use of effective cueing systems."

Clay (1993) recommends "practice in orchestrating complex processing on just-difficult-enough texts," stating that we need to provide students with "successful experience over a period of time moving up a gradient of difficulty of texts which can *support fluent and successful reading* [italics added]" (p. 53). The reading material must be well within the reader's grasp as the text, rather than the teacher, supports the learning of the student.

The Myth of Challenge

Jan has two sons who are learning stringed instruments. Her 14-year-old is learning to play the cello, and her 7-year-old is learning to play the violin. They take lessons from different teachers with very different philosophies of instruction. Jan's violinist, Natie, is learning with the Suzuki method, which increases difficulty with tiny increments and focuses attention on the processes of holding the violin, bowing, intonation, and so forth. Because the songs are simple, Natie can concentrate on multiple aspects of playing.

The 14-year-old cellist, on the other hand, has jumped into the deep end. Very early in his lessons, his teacher assigned him a difficult piece in the interest of giving him "something to sink his teeth into." Consequently, Christopher has struggled to get through the piece. Even though he has learned much about playing the cello, the difficulty of his practice material has compromised his ability to focus on integrating the many technical aspects of playing.

As a result, he has learned some inefficient habits that interfere with his progress. To a lay person, it would appear that Christopher is much farther along on the cello than Natie is on the violin. Christopher plays moderately difficult pieces and sounds pretty good, but to a knowledgeable cellist, it is obvious that he is struggling. He looks at his fingers, his hand positioning is inefficient, and his bow hold is incorrect. He would be much better off if his teacher had worked to solidify these and other foundational skills and processes with simple music rather than pushing him into something more difficult.

Musicians have since told Jan that a young string musician playing "Twinkle, Twinkle Little Star" with excellent posture, bowing, dynamics, and so forth will eventually surpass a student of music who is focusing on stretching to meet the short-term demands of getting through a challenging piece. The student working on process and simple music develops a feel for the whole, integrated effort, and this process becomes automated. The student consistently working at the extreme of his or her skills will usually adopt an inefficient, somewhat disjointed process, and eventually this inefficiency feels right to the student. Once this happens, even if the musician plays a simple piece, he or she will engage the same inefficient practices. So now, even if Christopher is playing "Twinkle, Twinkle Little Star," he holds his bow incorrectly and his posture is misaligned.

At some point, the student who spent a lot of time with challenging music has to back up and correct habits that he or she developed to compensate for efficient behaviors that he or she did not learn. For Jan's young cellist, she has had to back up, purchase simpler materials, find a new teacher, and support Christopher as he tries to break habituated tendencies that are already pretty solidified. This relearning is not easy in music or in reading, and it can be disheartening for students of either.

Similarly, in reading, students who work in material that is challenging develop compensatory practices that help them manage the difficulty of the text in the immediacy of the work. They may be able to get through the book, but they compromise their reading process. Once readers habituate these inefficient practices, they engage them even in the easiest of texts. Melody and Jan have both witnessed this time and time again.

Dueling Definitions of Instructional Reading Level

Consider the following examples of instructional-level text that we've created based on the story of *Goldilocks and the Three Bears*. The story contains exactly 100 words. The words in **bold** represent errors constituting 95% accuracy, the lower end of the limitations in Betts's definition of instructional level. Imagine that these errors represent problem-solving interruptions in the flow of reading and subsequent comprehension.

> Once upon a time, a family of three bears lived in a little **house** in the woods. One **morning**, the bear family left to walk, because their food was too hot to eat. A girl went into their house. She **found** the food and ate from the bowl that was not too hot or too cold. She sat in the best chair and **broke** it in two. She tried all three bear beds and went to sleep in Baby Bear's bed. When the three bears came home, they saw her in the little bed. She was **afraid** and ran home.

If we expand on this example, we can imagine that the hypothetical reader also made a couple of self-corrections. These self-corrections, although they indicate cue integration and strategy consolidation, interrupt fluency and comprehension as well.

With five errors and two self-corrections, one could reasonably argue that there is plenty of work for the student in the example above; there are five solid opportunities for the student to problem-solve making the text a reasonable challenge, and there are two opportunities for the student to reflect on efficient patterns of behavior. This work is sufficient (bordering on too much) for the student to learn something new. The following example, which represents more recent interpretations of instructional reading level, includes too many disruptions to a student's reading process, with the student reading at 90% accuracy:

> Once upon a time, a **family** of three bears lived in a little **house** in the woods. One **morning**, the bear family left to walk, **because** their food was too hot to eat. A girl went into their house. She **found** the food and ate from the bowl that was not too hot or too cold. She sat in the best **chair** and **broke** it in two. She **tried** all three bear beds and went to sleep in Baby Bear's bed. When the three bears came home, they **saw** her in the little bed. She was **afraid** and ran home.

Imagine again, that the student also self-corrected twice. Also imagine that the student is one of six students in a guided reading group, all of whom are making this many errors. This error volume may mean that students compromise their reading processes en masse while teachers struggle, usually with marginal success, to support them.

One might argue that the bottom end of Betts's parameters for instructional reading level overlap with the upper ends of the more common parameters, implying that students could work in easier texts without shifting the 90–95% definition. Teachers, however, like Mr. Stevenson, are under tremendous pressure to work with students in grade-level texts. So, many teachers understandably push these basal boundaries, placing students in the most challenging texts within instructional-level parameters. Because many teachers must report to parents or district supervisors the level at which their students read, giving students texts that fit the Betts definition of instructional reading level makes it look as if their students are behind.

Unfortunately, most teachers only have to report the reading level; more often than not, there is little reporting attention given to the quality of the reading process within that level (e.g., comprehension measures, fluency, self-correcting behaviors). Under such pressure, many teachers are inclined to let students work in texts they read with around 90% accuracy, general comprehension, and marginal fluency. Unfortunately, because of extensive work in these inappropriate texts, many students and teachers have a paradigm for how instructional-level reading looks and sounds, which they actually developed while working with frustration-level text.

Although historically educators have interpreted the term *instructional reading level* as the level at which students will benefit most from direct instruction in reading, we tend to think of it a little differently. Instructional reading level, as we have observed it, is the level at which a student has a strong enough reading process to learn from the work. So, rather than a source for teaching students how to use strategies, instructional-level text allows students who already have a repertoire of strategies strong enough to support them to attend to dimensions of the text that may be new to them (i.e., instructing themselves), whether it is new in terms of print, story, integration, or simply content.

The adoption of 90–95% word recognition as a guideline for instructional reading level seems to have spilled over from the Reading Recovery model, which is clearly a highly effective program for teaching students to read. Reading Recovery lessons, however, occur in one-on-one instructional contexts, which allow the highly trained Reading Recovery teacher to intimately know the readers' strengths and weaknesses. These individualized contexts are considerably different from classroom settings where teachers work with groups of students. We maintain that the demands of supporting one student who can potentially make 10 errors differ greatly from the demands of supporting four to six students who can potentially, and often do, make 40–60 errors. Furthermore, the spirit of Clay's work closely aligns with supporting the integrated processing of young readers over a drive to push them into "challenging text."

Clay's Smoothly Operating System

In *Reading Recovery: A Guidebook for Teachers in Training*, Clay (1993) writes about supporting students' reading behaviors as they develop a smoothly operating system for reading. She emphasizes the need to observe students and build upon reading behaviors over which the student has control. Clay writes,

> When one is having difficulty with a task one tries several approaches. As each fails one ceases to try them. The struggling reader has stopped using many strategies because he could not make them work. If you pitch the text at an easy level and you support him in using the things he can do you will find that he begins to try again some of these discarded strategies. (pp. 13–14)

In *Becoming Literate: The Construction of Inner Control*, Clay (1991) writes, "Learners do what they do well, and supported by this context they go beyond control they already have. *Therefore, the reader needs the kind of text on which his reading behavior system works well"* (pp. 214–215). She says much about working within what students solidly understand, moving them into new learning very slowly, and always offering massive practice to develop automaticity. Clay's (2005a) idea that real reading is an act of "fast perceptual processing" (p. 43) to the text is contrary to the model of guided reading instruction that allows students to pore over the text as they sort through a checklist of strategies.

Most of us define *strategies* as the tools we coach students to engage overtly when problem-solving, but Clay (1993) describes *strategies* as "these fast reactions used while reading" (p. 39). She continues, explaining that "monitoring and problem-solving strategies or operations going on in the student's head are more powerful than some of the weaker, overt procedures that teachers have encouraged students to use, like sounding out the word or reading on" (p. 39). We maintain that students cannot engage these fast, in-the-head strategies in texts that are difficult for them. Rather, they rely heavily on teachers to tell them which strategies to use and when to use them.

Clay (1993) does suggest giving students challenging texts, but we think her definition of *challenging* has been misinterpreted. She explains that text should be "just challenging enough," and "to achieve smooth integration of all the processing activities the teacher will sometimes need to drop the difficulty level of text until things are working well" (p. 52). So, guided reading is about learning the *orchestration* of behaviors rather than about the individual behaviors themselves.

The smooth integration of information occurs during the guided work, rather than students hobbling through a text leaning toward print or story and *then* smoothly orchestrating their reading when they move to independent reading. The reading process we expect students to practice in independence mirrors the reading process they are enacting during guided reading. If their reading process is fragmented, carried by the teacher, or uneven during guided reading, they are likely to carry this inefficiency into their independent application. Toward the end of supporting your efforts to help students develop smoothly operating systems for negotiating text, we offer the suggestions in the following section.

Working Through the Tricky Parts

Strategy #5: Teach Students From Books in Which They Can Practice a Balanced Reading Process

The inevitable difficulty of teaching students to read challenges us to balance the needs of individuals against the needs of the group. Like most literacy educators, we commonly administer an assessment and determine instructional reading level for our students. (We use the Betts 95–98% word recognition criteria.) Although these determinations give us quantitative descriptions of where our students can read comfortably, we look deeper to consider the qualitative ways students interact with text. That is, how does each student utilize print and story information?

You can base your grouping decisions on the numbers from your assessments and also consider the affective behaviors of the students. Set aside the level of the text and listen to the students read from a series of assessment materials. What is the most difficult level at which each student sounds like a reader who is putting all, or most, of the pieces together? What is the last level at which students can support themselves, the level just before their process becomes disjointed?

So, even if there are higher levels of text in which the students can stumble through 90% of the words correctly, perhaps only after a number of self-corrections (i.e., they have read less than 90% of the words without interruptions to comprehension), find the level where the students can actually integrate cues efficiently, even if that means letting them work within much easier text. This placement will allow you to observe the ways that students actually work through texts, the strategies that they can then carry into independence. Grouping toward process can also inform your decisions when half of a group is at one level and the other half is at another level. For example, if you have five readers with three reading at 96% accuracy in a Level F text and two reading at 96% accuracy in a Level E text, given that the students reading comfortably in Level E are frustrated in Level F, err toward the easier text and group all of the students in Level E. This adjustment will benefit all five students, because the reading process is the same in a Level E text as it is in a Level F text. If the students in Level E, however, are moved into Level F texts, they are likely to compromise their reading processes to meet the demands of the harder text, habituating compensatory strategies.

We have seen this process, which requires a fair amount of faith on the part of the teacher, pay off time and time again. When students who are consolidating cues smoothly work in slightly easier text for a while, they still make tremendous growth. It is not uncommon for students reading successfully within "just-difficult-enough texts" (Clay, 1993, p. 53) to make leaps of multiple levels between benchmark assessments.

Consider the following vignette:

Mrs. Ramen, a first-grade teacher in a school with a 95% poverty rate, decides to test this philosophy. This past school year, she measured guided reading instructional level according to Betts's 95–98% word accuracy, solid comprehension, and freedom from tension. The 15-minute guided reading session includes an introductory discussion and a picture walk before the first reading. After a conversation about the text, time still remains in the lessons for the students to reread a familiar text. Throughout the year, Mrs. Ramen retrains herself whenever she is inclined to move students into more difficult text. She makes sure each student has a smoothly operating reading process in a level before they move into more difficult text. This propensity sometimes means that she works with individual students to support particular strategies or that she revisits a strategy with the larger group.

Her restraint pays off; all of the students, based on Betts's parameters, started the year reading at Level A or B. At the end of the year, 12 could read at or somewhat above Level I and three struggling readers read fluently at Level F, all with 95–98% word recognition accuracy, solid comprehension, and strong fluency.

Contrary to common wisdom, the students do not steadily climb up levels, working through each level successively as the year progresses. Instead, the students linger in some early text levels long enough to establish an efficient reading process and consolidate new strategies. Due to Mrs. Ramen's attention to her students' reading processes, some students actually skip text levels. This decision pays off on the high-stakes reading test the students take in the spring; furthermore, they develop confidence and independence in their reading.

Table 5 summarizes the students' reading progress.

Table 5. Student Reading Progress Across the Year

Group	Aug.	Sept.	Oct.	Nov.	Dec.	Jan.	Feb.	Mar.	Apr.	May
1	A	A	B	B	C	C	D	E	E	F
2	A	B	C	C	D	D	E	E	E	G
3	A	B	C	D	E	E	F	F	F	H
4	B	C	D	E	E	E	F	F	G	I

As a Reading Recovery teacher, Melody witnessed yearly the truth of Clay's (1993) instruction to provide text that was "just-difficult-enough" (p. 53). One particular student from Melody's Reading Recovery experience exemplifies the power of easier text to promote a well-orchestrated reading process. Tonya, a second-round Reading Recovery student, had many inefficient reading habits that she learned in her early school experience. After 18 weeks of daily instruction, Melody had a fellow Reading Recovery instructor test Tonya to see if she could discontinue from the program. The proctor recorded the testing session and sent it to the district Reading Recovery director for approval.

A day later, Melody's supervisor informed her that, even though Tonya had scored at instructional reading level with 90% word recognition accuracy on Level J text, she could not discontinue from the program until her fluency improved. "Work on fluency for 2 weeks, have her retested, and send me the tapes," read the note at the top of Tonya's Level J running record. Melody initially disagreed with her supervisor. "If you only knew how far Tonya has come," reflected Melody, as she reached for boxes of leveled texts that would hopefully develop Tonya's fluency.

Contrary to common practice, Melody did not place Tonya in Level J books. Instead, Tonya read and reread daily for the next two weeks from familiar texts and novel texts that were in much easier levels, C through G. Much like Christopher, who had to move into much easier pieces of music even though he could play a few sophisticated pieces, Tonya had to work once again in easier text to practice and habituate a smoothly operating reading process.

With support, Tonya's reading process in simpler text evolved into a self-extending system. After two weeks and retesting, Tonya read a difficult novel, Level K text with 94% word recognition accuracy, solid comprehension, and strong fluency. Melody was amazed that Tonya had progressed so dramatically, even while practicing in Levels C through G, three levels below her "instructional" reading level. Melody's supervisor said, "Tonya sounds like a different student. Congratulations, Tonya has discontinued the program." Melody tacked those words to her bulletin board to remind her of the lesson she learned concerning the ways easy texts can actually be "just right" for helping students develop a smooth, integrated reading process.

Strategy #6: Increase Your Sensitivity to Reader Distress

Jan has worked with many students and teachers in guided reading contexts in the last 10 years and found it common for teachers, even those with tremendous literacy expertise, to work with students in books that are truly beyond their reach. In fact, the teachers who are most knowledgeable about literacy are particularly prone to placing students in difficult reading levels, because these teachers know how to scaffold to make the text more manageable. In the end, however, the teacher does most of the work, the text remains too hard for the students, and the students develop inefficient habits. Once teachers understand this cause and effect, they exclaim, "I can't believe I was doing that! I know better!" We have been guilty of this, too.

There seems to be some element of human nature, or perhaps it is increasing outside pressure, that drives us to push students. In so doing, we assume more and more responsibility for the work, and the students slip in confidence and skill. So, even if you are now conscious of the need to work with students in accessible texts, insidious tendencies toward agendas of pushing through the levels may still creep in. We offer Table 6 to help you recognize when a text may or may not be appropriate for your students.

To help you check yourself, we also offer this list, which is aligned to Table 6, of five questions you can consistently use to reflect on your guided reading lessons. These "five handy helpers" for guided reading teachers can help you automate certain processes for constantly cross-checking your understandings of guided reading against the behaviors of your students:

Table 6. Student Behaviors That May Indicate Appropriate Student-to-Text Match

Text That Is Too Difficult	Text That Is Just Right
Students are off task, nervous, or engaged in inappropriate behaviors.	Students are focused on the text during guided reading sessions and engage in conversations about their work.
Students read haltingly. Their reading may include excessive repetitions or self-corrections or require extensive teacher support.	Students sound like good readers most of the time, with occasional stops to problem-solve. Most problem-solving is independent.
The lesson takes more than 15–20 minutes, because the teacher has to instruct extensively. There is often frequent problem-solving.	The lesson lasts 15–20 minutes. Instruction is mostly (or all) around reflecting on what worked.
The teacher has to support all readers and cannot shift attention to administer a running record on one student or make notes about the lesson.	The teacher makes notes on the guided reading session and makes a running record on one student.
The teacher is frustrated and tired from extensive explanations and frequent prompting.	The teacher is quiet and listening for much of the session.

1. *How did the students feel?* If the students showed signs of tension as they worked through the text, the text may have been too difficult. Tension manifests in many ways: Students may fidget or wiggle in their seats, display excessive repetitions in their reading, or simply offer spontaneous deep sighs. A smoothly operating process should support the students in a successful reading experience. Did the students enjoy the guided reading lesson? If not, check the text level.

2. *How did the reading sound?* Was most of the reading smooth for the students? How often did the processes that should be mostly automatic in instructional-level texts demand the conscious attention of the reader? If the students had to stop to solve problems, were they mostly able to figure them out with minimal support? If the students consciously worked on more than 3–5% of the words, read laboriously, were unable to solve most problems independently, or struggled to understand the text, then it was probably too hard. Most guided reading should look

like a group of solid readers flying solo with their teacher waiting in the wings to catch, encourage, and observe them.

3. *How long was the session?* If you have to spend more than one day on the same work or are stuck in a text working on different processes on different days (e.g., a day to work through the words, a day to navigate the meaning, a day to practice fluency), then the text is too hard. If the text requires that you squeeze the entire gradual release of responsibility into guided reading, then you need to pick a different book.

4. *What records did you take?* If you were so involved with supporting the students that you were unable to take anecdotal records or administer a running record during the lesson, then the book was probably too hard. If the teacher shifts focus to documentation and the students' reading grinds to a painful halt with students operating at varying degrees of being stuck, then reexamine the text. You should be able to record one student's reading behavior without the reading processes of the other students falling apart.

5. *How hard did you work?* If you, the teacher, are saying "Whew!" at the end of a lesson and trying to catch your breath, then you may want to look at your text choice. If you are doing the heavy lifting of the lesson, then your students are probably missing valuable opportunities to practice their integrated reading process and may even be developing habits of dependency. More often than not, the students should be more tired than you after a guided reading lesson.

Internalizing these five questions can help you keep in check the natural tendencies toward oversupporting and pushing through levels that we all sometimes indulge. You might keep this list in your notebook for documenting your guided reading work and review it at the beginning of each lesson until it becomes an automatic part of your thinking.

Strategy #7: Select Guided Reading Texts Based on Student Reading Processes

Most of the critical planning of guided reading instruction rests in the teacher's text selection. This work involves considering the background knowledge of the group in terms of print and story. In addition, text selection requires us to consider our students' reading processes very thoughtfully.

Various tools exist for supporting teachers as they consider texts in relation to the readers in a group; however, most tools have a heavy print focus. Again, we do not suggest that you become casual about print considerations of a particular text. Rather, we suggest you become even more serious about story and integration considerations. Clay (1993) writes, "Choose the reading book very carefully. First of all take meaning and language into account" (p. 36).

To select texts toward reading process rather than simply by level adds a layer of complexity to the task. First, we need to understand each student's reading process in a given level. Jan has worked extensively with teachers and supported their use of a "visual vocabulary" to graphically represent the ways that students process information while reading. They represent the process by drawing the appropriate Venn diagram, like those we presented in the Introduction. As you consider which of these Venn diagrams represent each of your students, you can let these understandings inform your text selections.

Selecting Texts for Students Who Favor Story Cues. For a student who relies too heavily on story, teachers can select text that requires students to attend to dimensions of print. If only a few students have this challenge, the teacher may support student shifts from story to print in small-group, shared reading lessons, or individual reading conferences. In selecting texts that encourage print attention, teachers might consider the following questions:

- Are the print elements within the control of the student? Shifting attention is enough work. Once the student refocuses, will he or she be able to manage the print? You may need to move to even easier text if you are trying to help a student break a bad habit.
- Is the language of the text natural and within the student's control? Some texts that support increased attention to print sacrifice natural language structures for the sake of phonetic reliability. If you are using a story that is patterned with a particular word family, for example, make sure there are illustrations that add depth to the text and that the words are not nonsensical.

- Are the story dimensions of the text, as they align one-to-one with print, limited enough to require the student to attend to print? For example, a text with a picture of a black dog right above the words *black dog* will not encourage the student to access the print.

- Are the story elements of the text, particularly the illustrations, complete enough to support confirming, cross-checking, and even deep comprehension? Even though you want the student to shift some focus to print, you don't want to go to an extreme in the other direction. Always reconnect with other cues.

Selecting Texts for Students Who Favor Print Cues. Just the opposite of the reader we just described, some readers engage "sounding out" behaviors almost exclusively. These students need texts that push them to turn their attention to alternate cues. The following questions may help you select texts for students who rely heavily on decoding, even when it is not efficient:

- Are the story elements within the control of the student? Shifting attention from print is enough work for students. Once the student refocuses, will he or she be able to understand the story elements the text provides? You may have to move to even easier text if you are trying to help a student break a bad habit.

- Are there multiple story elements to support the student? For example, texts with a consistent pattern and a close picture–print match will present students with more than one aspect of story to which they can direct their attention. Consider availability of story aspects, such as rhyme, language structure, print–picture alignment, and repetitive patterns, and background knowledge of the student.

- How will the print support the student's efforts? This support may vary, depending on the student and the text. In some situations, using texts that are more difficult to decode will help the student shift attention to story elements that are not limited by the print. On the other hand, maintaining enough manageable print to afford confirming story cues is generally productive as it connects the student to a complete reading process.

Selecting Texts for Students Who Do Not Comprehend Deeply. Some students read texts superficially. They can answer basic questions (e.g., what did the boy eat?) and give a general retelling of the story, but they don't work to connect meaning across the text or to their own background knowledge. For these students, you might consider the following as you select texts:

- To what big ideas does this text lend itself? Select texts that have ideas within and around other ideas. If there is one right answer to the questions to which the story lends itself, the text may not be rich enough for the work.
- What does the story offer readers as they work to engage in a sophisticated reading process? Are there opportunities within the text to access different ways of thinking about texts? Can you think of comprehension questions that will encourage students to put together multiple strategies?
- How do the illustrations bring depth to the comprehension work? Even Level A texts can have complex stories embedded in the illustrations. Look for understandings that students can discover in the pictures, which teach them to think about the story as they are reading.
- Is the print within the control of the student? If figuring out the print interrupts the reading, students will not be able to efficiently attend to the meaning of the story.

Selecting Texts for Students Who Do Not Self-Correct. Some students leave many errors uncorrected, which may or may not disrupt their understanding of the text. Some errors may make sense on a sentence level but compromise the deeper understandings across the story. Either way, excessive, uncorrected errors indicate that students are not monitoring themselves as they read. The following list offers suggestions specific to particular error patterns:

- For students who make excessive errors that make sense on the sentence level, see the strategy for breaking inefficient habits in Chapter 5. For these students, it may be impossible to find a text that is on their instructional reading level in terms of word recognition until you break the habit. Then, you are likely to see rapid progress.
- For students who do not correct errors even when they don't make sense, teach them to ask themselves after each sentence, did that

make sense? Initially, this process is cumbersome and should be practiced in a shared reading context with a group that has similar reading patterns. Eventually, the questioning will become internalized and part of a student's reading process.

- In what ways will this text support behaviors that mirror the work of proficient readers? Basically, text needs to have print and story elements that are redundant, so students can learn to confirm one against the other.

This list is not exhaustive in terms of student reading processes and the ways they may inform your text selection. Rather, the list represents strategic ways of looking at guided reading texts through the lens of student reading. Examining texts thoughtfully in terms of story and print information in particular, as these support the specific reading processes of your students, will help you identify those texts that scaffold students.

Most important in terms of text selection, the guided reading book must be manageable for the readers. It is critical that we select a text that

is well within the child's control, uses words and letters he knows or can get to by using the present strategies. There should be a minimum of new things to learn if the teaching goal is the integration of all these aspects of the task. (Clay, 1993, p. 36)

By giving students texts they can manage, we nurture and solidify their abilities to integrate and consolidate various sources of information efficiently and practice the smoothly operating system that is the bedrock of learning to read.

Strategy #8: Clarify Confusions When Problem-Solving Efforts Prove Unproductive

Even when we know our students well and are highly knowledgeable about selecting texts that place instructional-level demands on them, we sometimes choose texts that don't match the needs of our students. It is impossible to always have a perfect match between texts and students. Generally, the result is simply that the students are trying to read books that are too hard for them. In these cases, teachers might change the guided reading session to a read-aloud or shared reading experience. Either of these are better options than carrying students through the text with excessive prompting, because read-aloud and shared reading do not fragment student reading processes or encourage students to work inefficiently.

If, on the other hand, you do decide that the book is generally appropriate for students, despite a temporary setback, don't let them remain stuck. When students are woefully mired in confusion, and you don't want to change the text altogether, go ahead and tell them what they need to know to move on to more productive work. It would seem that we are suggesting you engage in a practice that is in contradiction both with what we have already said and also with commonly accepted best practices. Our suggestion to tell students words when they are stuck or to explicitly clarify story confusion, however, is very context specific.

Because teachers understand the inverse relationship between telling and student independence, they are understandably adamant about letting students figure out the words. We suggest, however, that telling has received a universally bad rap. Sometimes, in the interest of saving time and avoiding frustration, we need to tell students what we wish they already knew. For example, students sometimes pore over a word, locked into some inaccuracy. There is something that they simply have wrong, and we keep prompting them to try again, giving them increasingly supportive clues. We may offer hints or suggestions, while the student continues to labor over the text. This happens with story work as well, as teachers work to support the inquiry and the higher order thinking that researchers define as critical to learning. Consider the following exchange during a guided reading lesson:

Ms. Wilson opens a guided reading lesson in her second-grade classroom by saying, "Does anyone know what a grader is?" The students shake their heads. "Are you sure?" she asks and waits in an effort to provide them sufficient wait time.

George responds confidently, "It is something you use for grades in school."

"What do you mean?" Ms. Wilson responds.

"Like a calculator. A teacher uses it."

"Hmmm," says Ms. Wilson. "So you are saying that a grader is a calculator that a teacher would use to figure out grades for a report card. That's interesting. Does anyone else have any ideas?"

No one responds.

"Let me give you a hint. It has something to do with road construction and big trucks."

There is a long pause while Ms. Wilson waits.

"Oh, I get it," says Chris finally. "A grader is something someone uses to give grades to the people who drive the big trucks. This is how they know if they are doing a good job on the road."

"Hmmm, that's interesting," says Ms. Wilson. "Anyone else have an idea?"

Imagine that this discussion continues until most of the time for guided reading instruction is lost. Ms. Wilson is trying to support the inquiry of her students. However, she is actually confusing them and taking up valuable time. The students have grabbed onto the only connection they have to grading and are trying to make it fit the current context. Ms. Wilson, although well intentioned, is perpetuating this confusion, which, even if she clarifies it at this point, may follow some of them into their reading of the text.

Because the students do not have sufficient background knowledge, they are unable to piece together the information efficiently. Inquiry such as Ms. Wilson's actually becomes a guessing game. Guessing, whether with print or story, based on no information or inaccurate information is usually unproductive and can perpetuate inefficient reading behaviors. Table 7 offers insights to support your decisions around whether to let students puzzle through problems or clarify their misunderstandings, so they can move on to more beneficial work.

There are no universal rules for telling or not telling. For each problem-solving experience, teachers weigh the momentum of the session, the needs of the student, and the demands of the text. Our goal is for students to develop fluency as they orchestrate the in-the-head processes they are developing. Grueling print or story work is inefficient and actually impedes our efforts. When students are desperately stuck, whether with story, print, or integration, tell them. If this happens frequently with a student, examine the level of text you are using, as it may be too difficult.

Table 7. To Tell or Not to Tell

When You Might Tell	When You Probably Shouldn't Tell
A student offers the same incorrect response even after redirection.	The student tries a new strategy, particularly if it incorporates a new cueing system or brings the student closer to solving the problem.
The print work seriously interrupts the meaning work.	You see the student searching in ways you think will be productive.
Story confusion leads students to reinvent the print, or print confusion leads them to make up the story.	A student, confused by story, is searching the print for clarification, or vice versa.
The student doesn't try anything, and other behaviors indicate that the text is too hard.	The student doesn't try anything, and other behaviors or your knowledge of the student indicate that he or she wants you to do the work.
The student makes a few failed attempts to find or correct the error after reading the sentence.	The student is in the middle of a sentence and makes an error.

Putting It All Together

In this chapter, we take apart one of the tenets of reading instruction that forms the cornerstone of guided reading: instructional reading level. We do not question these bedrock assumptions without years of thought and experience, and openness to your explorations of whether this truth holds up in your contexts. The paradigm shift we endorse is colossal, and therefore we encourage you to explore it aggressively before stepping into it.

We agree with Allington (2006), who asserts that "some children don't develop adequate fluency or rate of reading," because "they have limited reading practice in appropriately leveled materials" (p. 95), and "you can't learn much from texts you can't read" (Allington, 2002, p. 16). This chapter encourages you to reflect on students' reading abilities, knowing that the text, rather than the teacher, supports students as they develop a self-extending system. This reflection can give you faith as you consider text levels, skill in managing the chemistry between readers and texts, and patience as you nurture and watch for the coming of wonders.

QUESTIONS FOR REFLECTION
AND CONVERSATION

1. What are your understandings about instructional reading level, and how were they challenged or supported by this chapter?

2. Do you have students in guided reading groups who seem to be stuck in a particular level? In what ways might the level of the text contribute to their lack of forward movement? What will you do next?

3. What visual representations of the reading process presented in the Introduction illustrate the reading processes of your students? How do you know?

4. Are your students successful in guided reading? How do you know?

5. How do your students' reading processes influence the ways you select texts for them?

6. With what in this chapter do you agree? Why? With what do you disagree? Why?

A Literacy Story: Ms. Smith Sets Up Centers

Ms. Smith's first graders rotate through centers during guided reading. The students move to their first center after she calls out the names of students in her first guided reading group: the Level A group.

Ms. Smith doesn't call the group her "Level A group," but all the other students who are not in that group have already read the books that these four students now read. Ms. Smith recycles the leveled books throughout all her groups, which saves her a lot of time when she visits the book room. She just checks out books for the most advanced reading group and returns the books the least proficient reading group has finished reading. She keeps all of the levels in between and uses them with the various reading groups.

The students in Level A come to the reading table with their reading bags filled with books from previous days, which they have been taking home to read for homework. Ms. Smith sets a timer for 15 minutes, so everyone will know when to rotate centers.

After 15 minutes, the timer rings and the students reading from the Level A text stop momentarily while Ms. Smith tells the rest of the class to move to their next center. She's still not done with the first group, and you can see on Robbie's face that he really wants to get done with today's new book and get to his second center, computer games.

While Ms. Smith resets the timer, she wonders why these four students are having difficulty with this new book, because the other reading groups had no trouble when they read it for the first time. It takes 10 more minutes to finish the Level A book, because the students need assistance at different points in the text. Since just five minutes remain in the second block of center time, Ms. Smith decides to pull out sight words, because the students had such a difficult time with the book.

The timer goes off a second time, and Robbie, knowing he missed his first two centers, grabs his reading bag from under his seat and shoves the day's new book into it. Then, he grudgingly walks to his third center, math flash cards.

CHAPTER 3

Reconsidering Text Gradients

He fell into an ill humor...and such was his upset that José Arcadio Buendía himself relieved him of his duties in the laboratory, thinking he had taken alchemy too much to heart.

From *One Hundred Years of Solitude* by Gabriel García Márquez

We are classroom alchemists. We regularly exact a chemistry of students and texts that is more symbolic than scientific, more like imagining cloud animals than measuring temperatures, and we pull off the once again wondrous event of finding a rich match between a text and a reader. We manage to turn lead into gold—that is, match readers to books—but even so, our formulas are not consistently replicable and our solutions sometimes murky. The unpredictability of work we wish was wholly predictable sometimes leaves us weary and our students disheartened. It seems that we may take the alchemy of the text gradient "too much to heart."

One cornerstone of guided reading is the idea that we can determine a reading level of a student along a text gradient and then, using texts that are comparably leveled based on difficulty, we can match students to books in ways that facilitate their learning along a trajectory of increasing difficulty (Ford & Opitz, 2008b). On paper, this seems a marvelous idea, as systems of labeling and sorting sometimes help us manage and understand complicated processes. There are, however, a number of shortcomings in this system, as well as a few significant negative side effects.

Text Leveling and Pseudoscience

The science behind matching students to texts is actually a bit shaky. This work is based on the flawed premise that we can strictly define along quantitative parameters the relationship between a student and a book, and that this relationship will consistently bear out, reproducing itself as other students meet these leveled texts. In reality, we find that this assumption does not always hold up in application. Researchers argue that there are few solid understandings about the contributions of texts to beginning reading, partly because there isn't an acceptable method for validating leveling schemes (Cunningham et al., 2005).

In fact, we see a lot of logic in the work of Rosenblatt (2004), who suggests that the interaction between a student and a book varies greatly based on what the reader brings to the experience. Along these lines, DeFord, Lyons, and Pinnell (1991) explain that there are only text gradient *approximations* that serve as a guide rather than an inflexible sequence. They go on to explain that a "particular book may be appropriate for one child at one level but inappropriate for another child who reads at the same level" (p. 124). It makes sense to us that the relationships between students and individual texts are idiosyncratic and cannot be narrowly defined along levels. Nevertheless, text gradients are tremendously helpful. We rely on them to help us manage the challenges of teaching a lot of students to read.

Most teachers of guided reading understand that all texts on a particular level are not the same. Texts vary greatly along a host of traits. Furthermore, what one educator will describe as a Level D text, another will describe as a Level E, and still another may describe as Level C. Also, an array of student factors, such as background knowledge and motivation, can influence a student's interaction with a text. Clay (1991) writes, "Gradients of difficulty are essential for teachers making good decisions about materials they select for children to read but all gradients are inevitably fallible" (p. 201).

Although educators tend to understand this fallibility, in practice they often find students (and themselves) locked in a particular set of books that someone, who may or may not be more expert than they, has decided represents a particular level of difficulty. This strict definition of levels is sometimes due to the reporting requirements under which many of us work. It is common for districts to require teachers to note guided reading levels on report cards or other forms of documentation. We have even heard of situations in which students are retained because of their failure to meet the grade-level standards defined by guided reading levels.

Although most teachers clearly recognize the variability of texts within a guided reading level, most still won't teach a hard Level C text to students who are working in Level D readers. Even if an easy D and a hard C are qualitatively alike in many cases, teaching a Level D group in a C text implies regression, and teachers, students, and even parents systematically tick off the required successive progress through text levels. With an emphasis on "fine-gauged text leveling for reporting literacy outcomes" (Hill, 2001, p. 14), how do we, in the name of flexibility, explain to parents that a student reportedly reading at Level E may bring home a book at Level C or D?

From Leveling Texts to Leveling Students

The use of a text gradient to label texts paves the way for using this same leveling structure to label readers. Even more consequential, when using a text gradient, we tend to assume that the growth of the students with whom we work will mirror the logical sequence of increasing difficulty that is the backbone of the gradient system. The idea that readers move in precise ways through neatly defined stages and levels, and that they progress through these levels in systematic, chronological order, does not fit with what we have seen of beginning readers. In fact, Clay (1991) writes, "Fluctuations in performance, large leaps forward, movements backward in text difficulty to consolidate or recapitulate are movements to be expected under satisfactory conditions of instruction" (p. 216). Conversations about guided reading, nevertheless, are often about the systematic, step-by-step progress of a group. One drawback of these conversations is that, as we internalize categorical thinking about our students as readers, they may also internalize categorical thinking about themselves.

In the flurry of instruction, schedules, materials, standards, standardized tests, data teams, and students, we fall into a vocabulary of convenience. We say things like, "I'm working with my G readers today," or we talk in front of students about moving a group or a student "up" or "down." Statements such as these lead students to self-identify by text level. "I'm a J," says Emily to Jan when she walks into a second-grade classroom during a consultation with a school. So, the seeds of classroom competition are sown and nurtured, and we unintentionally set up a culture that is remarkably aligned with the groupings of "buzzards" and "bluebirds" that marked inflexible, homogeneous groups in the past (Ford & Opitz, 2008a).

Controlled Vocabulary Texts

Buzzard and bluebird groups were traditionally supported by texts that systematically control vocabulary, such as *The World of Dick and Jane and Friends*. There are volumes of print criticizing the "Dick and Jane" readers and other decodable texts. These texts are categorized as controlled vocabulary, because the words of the stories are carefully selected so that the beginning reader can manage them. They usually represent the most consistent phonetic patterns and repetition of a few sight words. Consequently, educators have criticized these books for their painfully dull stories.

Gradually, the field of reading wiggled out of the perceived straitjacket of these texts with their limited vocabulary (not to mention narrow representations of people) and eventually celebrated the arrival of leveled texts that were designed with consideration to both authenticity and readability. These "little books," which spilled into classrooms from Reading Recovery, then began to permeate education and influence instruction in largely positive ways. Teachers celebrated the relatively authentic language and the leveling system that made teaching beginning readers more manageable.

Although the differences in *The World of Dick and Jane and Friends* and *Mrs. Wishy Washy* are relatively obvious, *leveled texts* and *authentic language* are still a bit of a contradiction in terms. And the idea that "I see a red car. I see a blue car. I see a green car" represents authentic language invites question. Predictable texts are only *relatively* more authentic than the stories of Dick and Jane. This aspect, however, does not imply that these leveled, predictable texts are inappropriate.

In reality, anything that a beginning reader reads is necessarily going to have to reign in the complex demands of orchestrating and accessing multiple sources of information. The idea that the leveled texts we use to teach guided reading are not controlled vocabulary texts is a flawed one. The vocabulary of these books is, in fact, tightly controlled. They are just controlled in different ways than *The World of Dick and Jane and Friends* and toward different ends.

Guided reading instruction with early readers is primarily from texts that are leveled qualitatively, like the system described by Fountas and Pinnell (1996, 2005, 2007), and offer the earliest readers heavy support with story by using predictable language patterns. Both predictable and decodable texts are criticized for having too little of what the other has a lot of, whether story or print.

So Where Does That Leave Us With Text Gradients?

We are not arguing for eliminating text gradients from programs of instruction with beginning readers. They are necessary to navigate the terrain between "Dick and Jane" and *War and Peace*. Certainly, we cannot indiscriminately assign students reading material and expect them to work through the myriad of challenges they face in learning to orchestrate their reading processes. In making a case for mindfully and flexibly using text gradients, we are not advocating randomness or, even less reasonably, starting with the hardest texts.

There is nothing theoretically wrong with a text gradient. In fact, it is a useful tool for helping students develop smoothly operating systems for negotiating print. Text gradients also give teachers a skeleton around which they can organize instruction, monitor student progress, and engage in professional discussions. We believe that the texts for most beginning readers should have vocabulary that is necessarily controlled and that the growth of a novice in any area, from cello to rock climbing, tends to progress most solidly with practice in successively difficult material. The challenge, as is often the case in education, is maximizing the benefits of a text gradient while minimizing its shortcomings. Toward this end, we offer suggestions in the following section. Although there are many text gradients, we refer to the alphabetic leveling system presented in *Guided Reading: Good First Teaching for All Children* (Fountas & Pinnell, 1996) in the following discussion.

Working Through the Tricky Parts

Strategy #9: View Students' Reading Levels as a Range or Cluster

In many classrooms, teachers and students are locked into narrow definitions of reading and readability levels. We suggest, however, that educators can view text gradients through the lens of their limitations and work to employ them flexibly. To assist with this type of flexible consideration of the text gradient, we have found it helpful to view readability as a range rather than a narrow band. For example, we might refer to a student as working in a C–E cluster, rather than saying that the student is working in Level D. Broadening the reading level boundaries in this way gives teachers flexibility in text selection as they try to negotiate text and reader factors that vary from one reading experience to another.

Referring to ranges or clusters of levels rather than isolated levels also helps us focus on reading process rather than reading levels. Furthermore, this broader perspective minimizes the push to move up the levels. It blurs the categorical progress through an alphabetical or numerical trajectory. A student working in an C–E cluster is less obviously ahead of a student working in an A–C cluster than a student working in Level D compared with a student working in Level B.

Some of this viewpoint is semantics; a student working in texts ranging from C to E may very well spend the bulk of his or her time in Level D texts or in easy Level E texts. Nevertheless, the subtle difference in word choice gives teachers more freedom to pull in more challenging or simpler texts regardless of level, as these texts support instruction and often provide ways of thinking around flexible grouping.

Although considering reading level as a cluster of levels helps students and teachers think less categorically, it also helps parents consider reading process beyond level. One of the biggest challenges in dealing with guided reading levels, or any text gradient for that matter, is the difficulty associated with helping parents understand their limitations. Parents can unintentionally perpetuate labels, competition, and categorical thinking. Taking the emphasis off levels, as much as your school district will allow, and placing it squarely on reading process can help parents support their children's entire reading processes.

Strategy #10: Employ Flexible Grouping

When teachers broaden their understandings of the text gradient, it becomes easier for them to flexibly group students. One student may read from a text that is easier than he or she typically reads, and another student may read from a text that represents a skip in levels. Consider the following vignette:

Ms. Neher readies her students for readers' workshop, during which she plans to teach guided reading groups. She talks with them briefly about making personal connections with text, and then, as is their well-established routine, she sends them to get their browsing boxes and read independently. The students move efficiently to get books, stuffed animals, and folding chairs or pillows.

As the students get settled, Ms. Neher walks around the room quietly and taps on the head the students with whom she wants to work during guided reading. She plans to work with these students from texts that fit the qualitative definitions of Level E. Three of these students are part of a core group that generally works together.

One additional student, Evan, regularly works with a group practicing in more difficult texts, but recently his reading process has seemed a bit disjointed, and because Ms. Neher is knowledgeable about reading processes and observant of reading behaviors, she has picked up on subtle indications that he is experiencing some reading stress. So, Ms. Neher has pulled him to read with this group. Evan will still meet with his regular group when it gathers for guided reading the next day. He has no concerns that he is being moved down a group, as Ms. Neher groups her students flexibly and does not rigidly lock the work of any group into a level. Her grouping of students varies almost daily, and it is not uncommon at all for students to participate in more than one guided reading group.

Another student that Ms. Neher has pulled to join this group typically works from texts at Level C. Britanny, however, has really been poring over text and is very motivated to practice reading independently. Ms. Neher suspects that Britanny can skip a level, so she gives her the opportunity to attempt more difficult texts. If Britanny seems comfortable in this higher level, Ms. Neher will continue to let her work with both the group working in Level C and the group working in Level E, knowing that the extra practice will help solidify her balanced reading process. Finally, Terrance, who is normally reading from texts at Level J, joins the group, because the text for the day is about insects, and he is their resident entomologist. Ms. Neher knows that he will help lift the level of the group's story work that day.

Instructional moves, such as the ones that Ms. Neher demonstrates, show the subtleties of early negotiations with texts and with the systems we use to categorize them. Grouping students flexibly counters group stagnation and offers students of differing skill levels opportunities to collaborate and capitalize on one another's strengths (Guastello & Lenz, 2007). Working with students a little above or below the targeted level can be effective when it is the result of a thoughtful decision about the student's reading process and all of the places, not just the one, that a student might practice his or her smoothly operating system.

Strategy #11: Engage Independent Students in Tasks With Scope

In many classrooms, teachers use literacy centers to engage students in independent work while they teach guided reading to small groups, which may limit flexible grouping and flexible considerations of the text gradient. Furthermore, centers vary in their instructional value. Sometimes instructional density has to be compromised for the sake of independence so that a teacher can focus on the guided reading group without interruption from the students. The primary purpose for centers is often to occupy the other students while the teacher works with guided reading groups. There is typically a general assumption, perhaps valid, that the work in the guided reading groups is the most important work during this time.

We maintain that, even as early as kindergarten, students can learn to read independently. This independent work increases the value of student time away from the teacher. Independent reading takes less planning to support than centers (i.e., no one is rotating or setting up centers every week), and it is inherently valuable for benefits of extended practice in connected text. In *The Daily 5: Fostering Literacy Independence in the Elementary Grades,* Boushey and Moser (2006) offer specific suggestions for building student stamina for independent reading and for setting up independent reading as a complement to guided reading instruction. Their CAFE framework (Boushey & Moser, 2009) lends itself to flexible grouping for guided reading and supports the massive practice necessary for reading growth. In addition to sometimes holding less instructional value or requiring extensive teacher preparation, some literacy centers can limit teachers by holding them to particular patterns and rotations for gathering students for guided reading. If students have a particular sequence of centers through which they must work or are partnered with other students who will not be able to manage without the peer support, teachers are sometimes limited by the order and timing of teaching guided reading groups. This type of center work does not allow for the flexibility described in this chapter.

To pull any student for guided reading any time, even multiple times, students who are working independently must work on tasks that allow flexibility. Furthermore, as Clay (1998) suggests, independent work should be "tasks with scope" (p. 237). These are tasks from which students can benefit regardless of reading level or tasks that are inherently differentiated. Independent reading and writing, in a variety of permutations, as much as they are feasible given the levels of independence in a particular grade or class, are the most logical choice for this time. We include Table 8, which compares tasks with and without scope.

Student independence on tasks with scope requires that we teach students to attend to their work for increasingly longer periods of time. Although tasks with scope are ideal for fostering independence and engaging students in practicing complete reading and writing processes, we are not going to extremes. We appreciate that it is sometimes necessary to have students practice handwriting in isolation and that there are some valuable computer games that foster literacy. We simply suggest that we should offer the broader opportunities whenever possible.

Table 8. Tasks for Independent Learning During Guided Reading Sessions

Tasks With Scope	Tasks Without Scope
Rereading Big Books	Playing literacy games on the computer
Writing a story based on a pattern from a shared text or guided reading book	Handwriting practice in isolation
Independently reading from a browsing box	Completing reading comprehension worksheets
Using magnetic letters to make new words from a common rime	Completing a word search

Strategy #12: Use Controlled Vocabulary Texts Judiciously

We argue that, in the same way teachers using predictable texts are strategic about developing print understandings, teachers judiciously using decodable texts can be equally strategic about supporting student learning about story. Neither adjustment is easy, however. Teachers using predictable texts will often think they are doing enough work with the print, when in fact they may not, and teachers using decodable texts will often think they are doing enough work with story, when in fact they may not. In reality, the complexities of developing the systems inherently underrepresented in a particular type of controlled vocabulary text tend to be even more complicated than we might think.

Jan's 7-year-old son, Natie, is in first grade and is a strong reader. Last year he read a book from the "Magic Tree House" series each night until he had read them all, so Jan never imagined he would find a simple, controlled vocabulary text engaging. Recently, during the designated time when he reads to himself in bed each night, Jan heard him laughing uproariously. After this laughter continued off and on for half an hour, she stopped resisting the urge to interrupt him. "What are you reading?" she called out. "Dick and Jane," he responded. Curiosity piqued, she went to his room, where he effusively elaborated on the antics of Dick and Jane, characters he found hilarious and with which he was obviously connecting deeply. Perhaps it is not the limitations of predictable or decodable texts that are problematic, but the idea that we have to choose between them and then offer readers a narrow diet of one or the other.

Jan recently visited the classroom of a first-grade teacher whose room was bare, because she was packing. The entire school was moving so that the school district could make renovations to the school. With most of her books in boxes, the students were using retired basal readers for independent reading. For many educators, traditional basals with their decodable stories and limited vocabularies are not viable options for independent reading. These students, however, read dated, decodable texts with palpable enthusiasm, laughing aloud and sharing the parts of the stories to which they connected. One might reasonably argue that the students who consistently received reading instruction from texts with some level of predictability were working slightly different "muscles" by reading from texts that offered a little less opportunity for story reliance.

We have some concern that some readers might take our defense of decodable texts to an extreme. We do not endorse heavy doses of text with vocabulary that tightly controls print elements. We do, on the other hand, recommend that you use both text that controls vocabulary by managing story (i.e., predictable texts) and texts that control vocabulary by managing print (i.e., decodable texts). We rely more heavily on the former with students, as predictable texts allow us to more easily engage them in the work of thinking about meaning and are generally aligned more closely to the way students talk. Even so, judicious use of supplemental, decodable texts can help students who lean more heavily on story and are not efficiently using print.

Occasionally dipping into decodable texts requires students to shift their reading processes to accommodate the changing proportions of print and story support. This shift develops flexibility, which also helps readers as they adjust to read different genres. Work in decodable texts will help you see where student strengths and weaknesses exist within their understandings of print.

Furthermore, many decodable texts have strong story lines in the pictures. If you support students in exploring the big ideas in the illustrations, you counterbalance the heavy print work these texts demand. For example, in "Something Funny" from *The World of Dick and Jane and Friends* (2004), the text reads,

> "Look, Dick.
> Look, look.
> I see something funny.
> Come and see.
> Come and see Spot." (p. 24)

In isolation, the print in this text offers little opportunity for meaning work. The illustrations, however, complement the print in ways that give the reader a chance to engage a balanced reading process. In the pictures, Spot's ears are getting wet as he drinks from his water dish. He shakes his head and gets everyone wet. Sally notices that she uses a ribbon to tie back her hair and runs to get a ribbon to do the same for Spot. So, although the print elements of this text are quite tightly controlled, there is, in fact, a lot of opportunity to explore story because of the generous story support in the illustrations.

A word of warning: Not all decodable texts are created equal. "See Spot run" is more bearable and authentic than "The fat rat sat on that mat." So, even within our gentle endorsement of occasional and limited use of decodable texts, we recommend that you look carefully at the particular decodable texts you use. Select these texts as you would predictable texts by considering the relative authenticity of the language, the support of the pictures, and the opportunities to bring in story. Also, counterbalance them with texts that are controlled along other dimensions, so students develop some flexibility in their reading processes.

Strategy #13: Linger at Level E

After talking at length about narrowly ascribing to levels within a text gradient, we want to take a minute to do what may seem contradictory to our prior discussions: We want to talk about Level E specifically. We have found that, for students learning to read along the text gradient trajectory, Level E is a particularly critical point. Level E is generally the place at which students either take off with their self-extending systems solidly supporting them or flounder with habituated, inefficient processing. If students have successfully worked—and worked is the key here—to integrate print and story through Level E, then they are often able to move on to increasingly difficult levels of text smoothly, rapidly, and with less teacher support. It is as if the work of figuring out how the act of reading *works* takes some focused, periodically intense effort in the earliest levels. Once this act of reading is actually figured out, however, reading improvement is largely a matter of doing more of the same in increasingly difficult texts. See Table 5 in Chapter 2, which illustrates that Mrs. Ramen spent extended time facilitating her students' reading practice in Level E.

If, on the other hand, teachers scaffold students so heavily in Levels A–D that, when students get to Level E, they are there largely by the effort of their teacher and not by their own puzzling through the reading process, then each successive level becomes increasingly laborious, and the students often spend their time struggling in subsequent levels, while a smoothly integrated system eludes them. Level E can be a brick wall in the text gradient. If students rely so heavily on the predictable patterns of the texts and the tight match between print and pictures prior to Level E, then their reading process may fall apart when they meet the demands of Levels E and F.

Melody has seen this barrier in development with dozens of first graders, and Jan has seen this obstruction as she has watched beginning readers across whole schools: The students who do not have well-established, balanced reading processes at Level E tend to struggle increasingly as they get into more and more difficult text. Furthermore, they are likely to get stuck in subsequent levels. Teachers find themselves saying, "I have used every Level H book in the book room, and this group just does not seem to progress. What do I do now?" Students who do not establish their reading processes before Level E often plateau, much like Christopher's cello playing. Although he could play some difficult pieces, he stopped progressing, because he had skipped some foundational skills and understandings, and his cello playing process was disjointed.

To prevent such plateaus, we suggest two things: First, in the levels preceding Level E, work strategically to foster independence as students develop a smoothly operating reading process. This effort requires that you continuously draw their attention to the ways that print and story confirm each other. Second, spend enough time around Level E (i.e., in the Level D–F cluster) to make sure that students are balanced, independent, and successful. Time and time again, we have seen students who are efficiently accessing and integrating cueing systems at Level E move beyond students who were inefficient but working in Levels G or H. Students who are solid, balanced readers at Level E often skip levels as they move through the text gradient. Again, learning to read is less about level and more about the reading process.

Strategy #14: Practice Mindful Language

Our language betrays what we believe about students and about learning. Even more critical, the way we speak of students, reading, and learning influences the sense students have of themselves. Johnston (2004) writes, "Language, then is not merely *representational* (though it is that); it is also *constitutive*. It actually creates realities and invites identities" (p. 9). Although it is easier to say "She's a D," or "He's an F reader," such labels can stay with students. Furthermore, labels can powerfully influence the ways students think about themselves as readers. If we are not very careful, we may prime students for failure (Gladwell, 2007).

We promote, in ourselves and in our students, negative perceptions around reading when we talk to them about moving up a group or even celebrate reading progress by focusing on levels. Perhaps our celebrations should be around new problem-solving behaviors or demonstrations of independence. Noticing that a student confirmed print cues with story cues or that a student really searched for and discovered deep meaning in a text offers opportunities for substantive celebrations.

In professional conversations, practicing mindful language poses a particular challenge. When we are trying to communicate or solve a problem, it is hard to think before we say something about how our "low" group is doing or how we work with our "high" students. Again, focusing on reading process can help. For example, we might talk about our group that is not confirming print with story or our group that has a smooth reading process. In actuality, a group working from Level J in ways that don't integrate print and story is a low group relative to a group that is reading from Level E in ways that smoothly integrate cues!

For the purpose of helping you consider your language around text gradients, we include Table 9, which presents common language around levels and alternatives that are less convenient but more mindful of students. When we are mindful of our language, we are actually acting in mindful ways toward students. Adjusting our language is a

Table 9. The Language of Levels

Language That Limits	Mindful Language
"I need my E group to come over for guided reading."	"I need Molly, Susan, Kendra, and Marcos to come to the guided reading table."
"You have worked so hard on your reading and made so much progress. I have moved you up to the next level!"	"You have worked so hard on your reading. Let me tell you what I have noticed. When you get to a word you don't know, this is what you used to do..., and this is what you do now...."
"Your child is a D."	"Your child is reading from texts that range in levels from C to E. These are the kinds of strategies your child uses when reading and this is the way you can support him/her at home...."
"I don't know what to do with my low group. They are really stuck."	"I have some students who are not confirming print cues with story cues or vice versa. How can I help them?"

relatively simple idea that holds the potential for great benefit in student empowerment.

Putting It All Together

There are many benefits to using a text gradient to teach students to read. Unfortunately, there are also many challenges. The elements of traditional reading groups that are onerous to many of us are the very issues that can taint our guided reading groups today if we are not mindful of the ways we discuss and carry out the classroom work involving leveling books, students, and groups. Teachers are responsible for judiciously using the text gradient toward the end of helping students develop smoothly operating reading processes, which inevitably build confidence. We can celebrate the alchemy in our classrooms when golden matches between texts and readers are created from a text gradient with leaden limitations. All the while, we are careful not to take the text gradient "too much to heart," recognizing its fallibility with readers whose thinking and learning don't always follow scientific reasoning.

QUESTIONS FOR REFLECTION AND CONVERSATION

1. Who benefits from the use of a text gradient? Why? Who loses? Why?

2. How do flexible considerations of the text gradient inform your guided reading sessions?

3. What types of controlled vocabulary texts are you using? Why? How are you compensating for the limitations inherent in each type?

4. In what ways is the use of a text gradient helping you teach beginning readers more effectively? In what ways is it limiting you?

5. What vocabulary do you engage around reading levels and groups? How is it working for you and your students? How might you improve it?

6. With what in this chapter do you agree? Why? With what do you disagree? Why?

A Literacy Story: Jasmine Tries to Sound Out a Word

It is March, and Ms. Burns is working with a group of kindergarten students from a Level B guided reading text. With the whole class, she has been systematically teaching the students the sounds the letters make and how to blend them together. She tells the students that, when they come to a word they don't know, they need to "sound it out," and she has modeled and prompted this procedure for them consistently throughout the year.

During guided reading on this particular day, Ms. Burns listens to Jasmine read. Jasmine is stuck on the word *dog* in the sentence "I see a black dog." She dutifully pronounces each of the sounds, except that she assigns a long sound for the vowel and adds a short *u* sound to the end. Jasmine comes up with "dōg-uh."

Ms. Burns has read that telling students the words can cause dependency, so she does not tell Jasmine the word. Jasmine continues to say "dōg-uh," even though Ms. Burns prompts her to look at the alphabet chart to see the other sound for the letter ō. Despite her frustration, Jasmine neither hooks into the pattern of the text (e.g., the preceding page read, "I see a brown cat") nor notices the prominent picture of a black dog right above the word.

CHAPTER 4

Realigning With Balanced Instruction

Alphabetical ourselves in the rows of classroom desks,
we were forgetting how to look, learning how to read.

From "The Reader" in *Sailing Alone Around the Room:*
New and Selected Poems by Billy Collins

Many of us crossed the threshold of literacy with Dick and Jane, perfectly polished children constantly pointing and asking us to "Look!" And we did, as beginning readers learn to look; we looked closely at the words, understanding eventually that they could actually tell us something important, such as who loves us, what time our mother will pick us up, or what's on the menu. White (1993) writes, "When children get the idea that written words can tell them something absolutely horrible, half the battle of teaching reading is won" (p. 170). This authenticity is the essence of learning to read: climbing over the print, perhaps on the shoulders of Dick and Jane, to get to the "absolutely horrible," or comparably compelling, in the story.

However, these are less sequential learnings and more simultaneous discoveries. For decades, the common wisdom of literacy education was that students learn to read in grades K–2 and read to learn in grades 3–5 (Robb, 2000). The idea behind this view was that decoding is the necessary focus of early literacy instruction, the sound implementation of which places students in good stead for comprehending the content area reading that forms the cornerstone of the later grades. Although educators have generally moved beyond this idea, its undercurrent still pulls at our reading instruction.

It is no wonder that instructional practice tends to bend to print in the early grades, as researchers have made clear the prominent role of print in beginning to read (Pressley, 2000). There is certainly much truth to this idea that students must master the print system. One would be hard pressed to argue against the value of teaching toward automatic word recognition in the early grades; there aren't many students who can comprehend deeply but can't decode the words. Not surprisingly, the link between ease of decoding and comprehension remains well established (LaBerge & Samuels, 1974).

It is not our intention in this chapter to question attention to the visual system in work with beginning readers. On the contrary, we believe very strongly in explicitly teaching students about print. Our premise is simply that story needs equal attention in the early grades. We need to teach even our youngest students to think of reading as meaning making and to act on texts in sophisticated ways to access these meanings.

The Reading Debate

The debate over whether early reading instruction should focus on print systems or meaning systems has long claimed the attention of many passionate reading experts. There seems to be a need among educators to decide that either print or story is the most important aspect of learning to read. As these debates influence classroom instruction, they may translate into extreme practices that either lean hard into phonics instruction or pull away from it. Inevitably, instruction squarely on one side or the other of this debate subsequently falls short and eventually propels the field of reading in the opposite direction. Then, of course, the pattern repeats itself.

Information Systems as Dependent Partners

Educators involved in early reading instruction can systematically consider both of these aspects of learning to read to help students develop proficiency with print and story and, most importantly, to thoughtfully use them to develop understandings in the other. Print and story are parts of a larger, united whole; one just isn't complete without the other. To think of them separately is like someone saying he or she is really great at balancing on a seesaw. You can't actually balance on a seesaw, however, without a partner, and you can't be great at seesawing by yourself. Although conversations about just one side of the seesaw may help one or the other partner to improve, the real act of balancing on a seesaw doesn't take place unless both partners climb on the equipment and work together. Comparably, print exists only in relationship to its significant other, story, and vice versa.

An Overemphasis on Print

In the vignette that opened this chapter, we presented a student, Jasmine, who relies too much on the information she gets from print. Consider Figure 2 in the Introduction, which illustrates print dependence. Although Jasmine is not automatic with letter sounds and patterns, she thinks these are her only option for figuring out unknown words. Students who rely too heavily on visual information are usually taught phonics in isolation, even within the context of reading. That is, even when these students work in connected text, they act as though they are working with the phonetic elements in isolation, and their teachers almost exclusively prompt them toward print. The behaviors they develop when practicing sounding out in isolation carry over into the reading work in ways that mirror decoding words out of context. So, when Jasmine reached a word she did not know, she tried to figure it out simply by trying to decode. She did not access the picture or repetition at all to help her figure out the word or to check her approximation.

As stated previously, there is value in systematically teaching print in isolation for the sake of working on particular skills that readers must automate. In terms of the seesaw analogy, this practice would be like having the individual partners do leg exercises or work on timing. In terms of reading, work with isolated elements of print can be valuable, as students must not only know all these elements but also must be able to use them automatically. However, if isolated work in print is overemphasized and not thoughtfully reunited with story, students can develop inefficient reading processes, which become difficult habits to break.

An Overemphasis on Story

On the other hand, in some classrooms, teachers explicitly teach students to rely almost exclusively on story to figure out the words, using context or structure excessively. Consider again Figure 3 in the Introduction. Students who receive little instruction in accessing print often default to the more accessible elements of story. Repetition in the text and a strong match between the words (i.e., print) and the pictures (i.e., story) support students as they learn to read.

However, if their attention is not intentionally brought to print and the ways it aligns with story, students can become overly dependent on illustrations, context, or structure and, once again, develop inefficient reading processes. If Jasmine had accessed story by looking at the picture of the black dog and said "puppy," she would have been relying on story at the expense of print. Her error would have made sense, but her lack of attention to print would reflect an inefficient reading process.

As with print, there is tremendous value in isolating story work. Often, this isolation occurs in the context of read-aloud when we teach students to focus on the language and the deepest meanings of a story. However, students with large vocabularies and inadequate letter–sound knowledge are limited in the progress they can make. Once again, it is a matter of plugging the student learning in regards to story into the full reading process and practicing the work of letting print reinforce what story is telling us, and vice versa.

Thinking Deeply About Story

This concept of teaching even very young students to think deeply about the meanings of stories while focusing on print is not a revolutionary idea, but it can be hard to pull off in the classroom. How might we teach our youngest readers in ways that develop the thoughtfulness we long to see in later grades? Calkins (2001) writes, "If we want to help all our children think deeply about texts and live comfortably in the world of ideas, then won't we want to introduce children to this habit of mind from the very start?" (p. 13). However, this arguably common sense does not easily translate into instructional practices with texts that read, "I see a brown cat. I see a black dog."

Despite the fact that prominent literacy educators (Clay, 1993, 2002; Fountas & Pinnell, 2006; Miller, 2002; Routman, 2003) have espoused the idea that we need to teach meaning in the early grades, instruction in discovering the deepest meanings of a text is often elusive in a guided reading session with beginning readers. Our exercises in comprehension tend to be limited (e.g., who are the characters in the story?), which may actually develop readers who attend to story superficially. Thus, our practices may be reinforcing and perpetuating the very reading habits that we have been trying to avoid. Applegate, Applegate, and Modla (2009) write that their interactions with university students and professional colleagues have revealed a pressing concern that that there is "an overemphasis in their schools on the development of oral reading indicators such as rate and accuracy without an accompanying emphasis on comprehension" (p. 512). We have certainly observed this trend as work with Response to Intervention pushes educators to focus on easily quantifiable reading behaviors.

Many educators have long thought that they have been teaching students to comprehend in guided reading groups; however, we maintain that we teachers of guided reading need our work with young readers in the area of story to go much deeper much earlier while maintaining a steady instructional interest in print. Otherwise, as Diller (2007) suggests, we run the grave risk of simply teaching students to decode when we think we are teaching them to read. So, our challenge becomes teaching beginning readers to decode *while* teaching them to comprehend rather than inadvertently teaching them to decode *instead* of teaching them to comprehend. To support your efforts to teach all students in ways that develop proficiency with both print and story, we offer these suggestions.

Working Through the Tricky Parts

Strategy #15: Engage All Students, Regardless of Instructional Reading Level, in Thinking Deeply About Story

One aspect of guided reading that we constantly explore is the ways that our questioning can push students to engage comprehension strategies. For example, Melody recently taught a guided reading lesson to a group of students using *You Can't Catch Me!* by Alison Hawes. Melody worked with Jan to consider the ways she could push the comprehension of her students by asking a question that demanded that they consider the text deeply and synthesize information across it. This approach differs vastly from traditional instruction, which has consisted of "a series of questions that emphasize right answers and single interpretations" (Fountas & Pinnell, 2006, p. 9).

In the text, the children play a game. Because the characters in the book chase and tag each other, the students in the guided reading group assumed that they were playing tag. However, Melody said to them, "I want you to read carefully. If you were on the playground playing this game, and a new student came to school, how would you explain it?" This question proved to be a powerful prompt for Melody as she encouraged the deep comprehension work of her students.

Melody's question required that the students interact with the story in ways that engaged multiple comprehension strategies. Of course, the students had to negotiate the bottleneck of the words; however, their attention to story supported this effort. Ultimately, they had to synthesize the text, connect it to their background knowledge of tag, summarize for the sake of the hypothetical new student, and clarify their misunderstandings.

Such comprehension instruction that honors the multidimensional nature of comprehending goes a step beyond comprehension work such as "Today I want you to make a prediction." We certainly are not saying that one should never teach to specific strategy work; we simply maintain that the complexity of reading demands that the heart of our work ask students to be active with their entire reading process rather than focus on some detail of it.

To ask a "big" question, such as the one Melody used, requires students to think about meaning on a text level, rather than on a page or sentence level. The more students begin to reflect on big questions, the more they begin to approach text thinking about big ideas. Table 10 offers suggestions for language that pushes comprehension to deep levels. To question students during guided reading in the ways suggested earlier in this section requires thoughtful planning. Teachers must select texts that

Table 10. The Language of Comprehension Instruction

Little Questions	Big Questions
What houses did each little pig build?	How are the pigs' houses different? Why did the writer have the third pig build the brick house instead of the second pig?
What did the wolf say before he blew down the houses?	Why did the wolf say the same thing at each house?
What happens at the beginning, middle, and end of the story?	What did the pigs learn from their experience?

offer opportunities to push students to think. Big questions support guided reading sessions rather than limit guided reading to the boundaries of a specific lesson, because they invite conversation and exploration.

How can we ask our beginner readers questions that will engage deep thinking that requires them to integrate a number of comprehension strategies when the early levels of text contain limited or controlled vocabulary? The answer often lies in the illustrations within the text. If a picture is worth a thousand words, then in guided reading, a picture is worth the thousand words the beginning reader cannot yet read.

In early texts, the pictures are the vehicle for communicating the complexity of story, complexity which authors increasingly communicate through words as texts move up a gradient of difficulty. Our efforts have been toward helping students learn processes for accessing these complexities in the same ways, whether they are gathering them through the pictures or through the words. Fountas and Pinnell (2006) write, "When we believe that reading is a process of making meaning using *all* [italics added] available sources of information, we keep readers connected to the meaning of texts all the time" (p. 545). Sophistication in the pictures can offset the simplest of texts and allow readers opportunities to develop the deep thinking behaviors we want them to habituate. When we are encouraging the habit of mind of practicing deep thought about a text, we can utilize every integrated aspect of the text.

For example, consider *The Ghost* by Joy Cowley (see Figure 6). In this book, readers may notice that the page-by-page sequence of rooms is the path the child in the story follows in search of her parents. The readers may also work to figure out why the cat on page 5 is frightened. To arrive at either of these understandings, students must make inferences and connect information across the text, again engaging in connected processes rather than an isolated strategy. The biggest idea in this text, at least the one students most love to discover, is that the illustrations are drawn from the literal point of view of the child in the story. They are all in the shape of the eyeholes the main character has cut into a paper bag to make a ghost mask.

Conversations about the inferences students must make to understand the text deeply push students to approach the work actively, giving them a purpose for their reading that prompts integration of information. This active stance supports students as they think about the text in

Figure 6. Illustration Extends the Meaning of the Print

I see the chairs.

6

Note. From *The Ghost* (2nd ed., p. 6), by J. Cowley, 1990, Bothell, WA: Wright Group.

sophisticated ways and begin practicing the thinking work we want them to habituate and carry into the rest of their lives.

Strategy #16: Teach Students to Look Closely at Print, but Not at the Expense of Story

Reading relies on the medium of print, but students must learn how to access visual information without becoming overly dependent on it. Toward these goals of balance and integration, teachers can teach students conventions of print throughout the gradual release of responsibility. Having a specific time each day within the literacy framework to focus on the conventions of print can inform the work with connected texts in shared, guided, and independent reading experiences.

Consider this story, which illustrates a focus on print that shifts to reconnect print with story:

During guided reading, Reginald, a first-grade student, misreads the sentence "She saw a little, brown hut" as "She saw a little, brown hat." His miscalculation makes sense at the sentence level but not in the context of the whole story. Because he is relying on story on a sentence level, he does not notice the error.

His teacher, Ms. Nichols, asks him to "Try that sentence again," which prompts him to look at the print more closely. Reginald is automatic with all of his letters and sounds, including vowels, but he is not looking closely at the whole word. This time when he reads, he again says, "She saw a little, brown hat." He then pauses a moment, quickly self-corrects, and says, "Hut." He then immediately goes back to the beginning of the sentence and reads, "She saw a little, brown hut." Then, he continues reading the rest of the book.

As other students have demonstrated patterns of errors with vowels, Ms. Nichols decides to address in isolation their attention to print. The next day, she asks the whole class to read out loud a list of words that are graphically similar to *hat*:

hit–hut
hot–had
hit–hat
hat–hut
hut–hit
hot–ham

Ms. Nichols tells the students that she wants them to look closely at the print. Next, she makes a game of giving individual students the opportunity to read the list as quickly as they can and is careful to give Reginald a turn, as well as others who demonstrate a tendency to overlook the middle of the word in connected reading.

After all the work in isolation, Ms. Nichols asks students to read a list of sentences that all have words that are graphically similar to *hut*. Again, she asks the students to read in unison. Finally, using a document camera, Ms. Nichols presents the text from the previous day's guided reading lesson, and the whole group engages in a shared reading of the text. She also intentionally makes an error that makes sense on a sentence level but not with the larger context and engages students in conversations about thinking about the whole story as they read.

During guided reading, Ms. Nichols listens to Reginald to see if he is utilizing print more efficiently and paying attention to meaning across the whole story. When he reads with accuracy, she prompts him to reflect on his success.

Exercises such as in this story can help students begin to develop automaticity with print. Tools such as magnetic letters, pocket charts with words and sentences cut apart, and whiteboards support teachers as they reinforce print throughout the gradual release of responsibility.

Finally, returning to the story that Jasmine was reading, if a student correctly says that the troublesome word is *dog*, you can ask the student to blend through the whole word as a way to check it and then have her reread the sentence. When we ask students to take the time to look carefully at words with which they have problem-solved and already demonstrated accuracy, rather than simply telling them they are correct, we help them practice within their strengths. Practicing in the known puts them in a secure place to tackle the unknown successfully, or make what Clay (1991) refers to as "frontier attempts," which extend their control into new territory (p. 214).

Strategy #17: Encourage Students to Talk About Their Thinking, but Not Too Much

As students actively search for meaning in the text or work to answer questions that push them to comprehend across the story, it is often worthwhile to ask them to explain how they figure out some story aspect of the text. Likewise, as students tackle challenges with print, they can benefit from articulating their thinking before and during the attempt. We think these metacognitive moments are most valuable when they refer to the ways students are integrating sources of information.

Thus, we are not suggesting that you prompt for the particulars of a reading process (e.g., who made a connection? what sound did you say?). Rather, we return to our original argument that sometimes the best way to capture a complex process is through simple methods. So, we suggest a more global question to prompt a reader's reflection on the reading process in its entirety. For example, you might ask a student who has solved a problem, "How did you figure that out?" Embedded in the response, a student might include a number of story or print subprocesses.

For example, consider the book *In My Room* by Ron Bacon (see Figure 7). For this little text, a teacher might reasonably ask a group of readers an inferential question that requires them to consider information across the whole text. To put even more responsibility for the thinking task on the shoulders of the readers, a teacher might simply ask students

Figure 7. Illustrations Across the Text Help Students Understand the Print

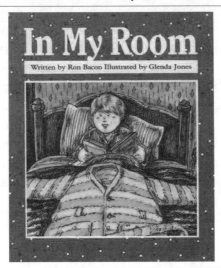

Note. From *In My Room* (cover), by R. Bacon, 1997, Crystal Lake, IL: Rigby.

to read the story carefully, because there is a really important idea hidden in the words and the pictures. Once students have responded to either of these prompts, or something similar, teachers can take the thinking a step further and ask students how they figured out the answer. A student who has had practice with thinking deeply about texts might respond as follows:

> Well, there were a lot of animals in his room, and I couldn't figure out where they were coming from. He was in his room with the lights out. Then, when his mother came in, the lights were on, and the animals were gone. So, I looked back, and the animals were his clothes. You see! His belt was a snake. And look at the front, there is the bathrobe. It has stripes like a tiger. He got scared, and then his mother turned on the lights, and there were no animals in the room.

In this reflection, a student engages in thinking about a number of active strategies that are visible and, in all likelihood, a number that are in the head. This thinking aloud informs students' future work with story and lets them model for each other the ways that reading works.

Although we maintain that it is useful for students to talk about how they figured something out, we don't think you should have students think aloud once they demonstrate automaticity with a strategy. Nor do we think it is particularly productive to get hung up on labeling strategies in a certain way. If a student is efficiently clarifying, there is little need to expend a lot of energy on labeling the strategy. The student in the previous scenario would not comprehend any better by matching labels to the various strategies. We are not saying that students cannot handle the vocabulary of strategies; we are just saying that the labels are not the point. If students learn them quickly, and the labels facilitate conversations about the ways that text works, then labeling strategies can be valuable. On the other hand, when students are penalized for inaccurately labeling their thinking, or when instructional time is largely spent on teaching and clarifying labels rather than engaging with connected text or actually practicing strategies, then our energy is misspent.

Putting It All Together

Literacy researchers and practitioners have long debated the roles of print and story in teaching reading and in learning to read. We suggest that you remove yourself from these discussions of extremes and embed your literacy instruction in solid understandings of the ways you want your students to integrate information from both story and print. If you constantly evaluate your instructional decisions by asking yourself, how will this affect the ways my students interact with connected text? you are likely to make wise choices in terms of supporting your students in developing proficiency with print *and* story.

In this chapter, we endorse work that isolates various aspects of the reading process, both in story and in print, but only toward the end of reassembling the process and making it smoother. We may ask the reader to "Look!" closely at print, directing his or her attention to the letters, their form, their order, and their place on the line, but we are intentional about circling back to story for the horrible and wonderful ideas it offers, as they are the most compelling reason to assume literate lives.

QUESTIONS FOR REFLECTION AND CONVERSATION

1. In what ways do you support students as they learn about print *and* story?

2. What do most of your students do when they get to an unknown word? What does this tell you about your instruction?

3. How do you know when your students comprehend a text deeply? Why does this matter?

4. How do you know whether to address an aspect of print or story in isolation or in context?

5. How are you connecting print and story work across the gradual release of responsibility?

6. With what in this chapter do you agree? Why? With what do you disagree? Why?

A Literacy Story: Ms. Duncan Teaches Her Students to Read

Ms. Duncan, a first-grade teacher, knows the importance of immersing her first graders in print. Every year, parents request her as the teacher for their rising first-grade son or daughter, because, at the end of first grade, Ms. Duncan's students can always read the words in second-grade text.

Ms. Duncan teaches print through the gradual release of responsibility. Each day, she reads a Big Book with the class and supports them as they identify various print elements in the text. The next day, she uses the same text after copying it on a chart, so students can work with print without the distraction of pictures.

With small groups each day, she listens to individual students read and makes notes about their accuracy. She assigns homework and follow-up practice based on the patterns of word recognition difficulty students display. Ms. Duncan's students consistently learn to read with fluency. They can also tackle an unknown word confidently and take it apart phonetically.

At the end of first grade each year, she reviews her students' reading progress throughout the year and usually finds, much to her satisfaction, that most are decoding text at the second-grade level. In the fall, however, the second-grade teachers are less enthusiastic about receiving students from Ms. Duncan's class. They know they will have to work particularly hard to compensate for the comprehension work the students didn't do in first grade.

CHAPTER 5

Recommitting to Integrated Processing

The Human Being is a repairing animal. <u>Homo sapiens</u> is also <u>homo reparans</u>.

From *Repair: The Impulse to Restore in a Fragile World* by Elizabeth V. Spelman

We are beings intent on salvage. Our minds solve problems, our hands and our hearts mend fences, and our cells keep fixing us. Poet Carol Lynn Pearson (1992) writes, "But cells die / And every seven years we are new" (p. 52). From the inside out, we are correcting and reclaiming, much like a reader who works at building and rebuilding the text, self-correcting along the way, aiming for repair that brings understanding.

In the past 20 years, reading instruction has evolved to support young readers by scaffolding the print, meaning, and structural systems, giving students mostly accessible words with which to problem-solve and somewhat authentic stories about which to think. With the translation of Clay's reading research to small-group instruction in the form of guided reading, reading instruction has gotten as close to considering the student's whole reading process, as opposed to subskills, as it ever has. Such efforts to consider the relationships between reading cues and students' whole reading processes have contributed to tremendous progress in literacy education. When we work with students to integrate information from story and print, confirming and cross-checking strategically, we support them as they establish balance, as described in the Introduction.

The Continuing Curriculum

Jan spent six years coaching literacy in an elementary school. She was charged with supporting all aspects of literacy instruction in kindergarten through fifth grades. Initially, she envied K–2 and 3–5 literacy coaches who were able to concentrate their studies and their energies on the lower or upper elementary grades. As she gained more experience, however, she began to understand the powerful implications of a connected curriculum and the ways that students develop habitual reading behaviors in kindergarten that can follow them throughout their elementary careers.

We have noticed, not surprisingly, that students who have difficulties with reading in kindergarten and first grade often are the same students who experience difficulties in third grade. It does not take a quantum leap to realize that the students who master story in kindergarten may be more likely to read for meaning in later grades, and students who master print in first grade may have better fluency in fifth. The simplicity and elegance of connecting the ways we teach to the ways students read make us feel once again like those fish scientists discovering water. Our realization is this: From the moment they enter elementary school, every encounter students have with text should involve thoughtful interaction with print and story that translates into deep understanding.

A Word About Strategies

Whereas some reading research and practitioner texts focus necessarily on isolated strategies (Harvey & Goudvis, 2007; Miller, 2002), researchers consistently point out that, in the end, reading is a system composed of a host of interwoven processes. In reality, comprehension instruction should, as much as it is able, teach students to integrate these strategies (Pressley, Johnson, Symons, McGoldrick, & Kurita, 1989). Researchers note, "What became apparent was that skilled reading did not involve the use of a single potent strategy but rather orchestration of cognitive processes" (Brown, Pressley, Van Meter, & Schuder, 1996, p. 18). So, although research has consistently demonstrated that strong readers use particular strategies and that less skilled readers can learn these strategies (Duke & Pearson, 2002), we want our instruction to, as much as possible, teach a process rather than a particular text, to connect to an interwoven system rather than focus on isolated strategies.

When we ask students to activate an entire reading process and position them in an active stance as they interact with the text, we honor the complexity of reading. As Fountas and Pinnell (2006) suggest,

Our goal as teachers is to enable readers to assimilate, apply, and coordinate *systems of strategic actions* without being fully aware that they are doing so. Readers' attention must be on the meaning of the text rather than on how to make their brains perform a particular operation. (p. 45)

Work with story and print is part of a larger system for integrating information and can be informed by the complex behaviors of proficient readers. Toward this end, we offer the following recommendations to support your students as they develop understandings about the ways print and story work together in a smoothly operating system.

Working Through the Tricky Parts

Strategy #18: Teach Students to Notice the Ways a Text Supports Itself

In shared, guided, and even independent contexts, you can show students the ways that text is redundant, giving the readers more than one avenue for solving problems. Imagine, for example, using in a shared reading situation the story with which Jasmine was struggling in Chapter 4. The teacher might ask the students to talk about the ways they can figure out the troublesome word *dog*. One student might offer insight into the print. Then, the teacher might say, "So, you used the print to figure out the word *dog*. How can you check using different information?" Then, another student might point out the picture of the dog. This confirming is rather like the way students check their addition by subtracting and vice versa.

Taking the process of cross-checking and confirming information to a conscious level is actually focusing on a subprocess *in context*. It is breaking apart the reading process and making explicit the actions that are usually in the head. The more you support students' understanding of cross-checking through modeled and shared contexts, the more you are likely to see students cross-check in guided reading.

As teachers, we are often so excited about a student figuring out a word that we respond by saying, "You got it!" What if we instead asked with a straight face, "How do you know that word is *dog*?" and then, "How else do you know?" When educators pose such questions to students, Clay (1993) asserts that they invite "the child to examine his own behaviour" (p. 43). We question to raise a student's self-awareness and to begin developing habits of comparing and contrasting information within the text. Work that requires students to practice reading as an integrated process helps them develop balanced processes for solving problems, confirming their solutions, and reclaiming comprehension. Table 11 offers language for supporting students in integrating information.

Cross-checking behaviors, such as those supported with the language in Table 11, are logically taught during shared reading. Shared reading contexts prime the application of these behaviors under the watchful eye and thoughtful scaffolding of the teacher during guided reading. Teaching the strategies in the larger groups during shared reading also gives us some economy of instructional time. Such preparatory

Table 11. Using Redundancy in Text

Print-to-Story Language	Story-to-Print Language
Text reads, "I see a black dog." Picture shows a black dog.	
Student problem-solves *dog* and rereads, "I see a black dog." You say, "You used the letters to figure out *dog*. How can you check to see if *dog* is right?"	Student reads, "I see a black dog." You say, "You used the picture to figure out *dog*. How can you check to see if *dog* is right?"
Student reads, "I see a black d_____." You say, "You used the first letter. What else can help you?" or "You said *d*. Now what should you do?"	Student reads, "I see a black puppy." You say, "You used the picture to make the sentence make sense and sound right. What else do you need to check?" or "How do you know if that is right? How else do you know?" or "Try that again."
Text reads, "The cat has a blue bow." Picture shows a cat with a blue bow on its head.	
Student reads, "The cat has a blue bow." [rhymes with cow] If the student stops and notices that something is wrong, ask, "Why have you stopped?" and "What can you use to check? What else can you use?" If the student does not stop, say, "Try that again" or "Find the problem."	Student reads, "The cat has a blue bowl." If the student stops, ask, "Why have you stopped?" and "What can you use to check? What else can you use?" If the student does not stop, say, "Try that again" or "Where's the problem?"

work enables teachers, during guided reading sessions, to utilize the redundancy of text through broad prompts that invite students to solve their own problems.

Strategy #19: Prompt Less and, When You Do, Prompt Toward Integration

Scaffolding is arguably the backbone of the gradual release of responsibility. It is possible, however, to scaffold so much that students have very little responsibility in the work. Interestingly, a synonym for *scaffold* is *gallows*. It seems that the very platform that should support students' reading processes can actually hang up these processes if we are not attentive to helping students develop independence in reading.

Students are more successful when we teach from what is within their realm of control. Clay (1998) writes,

> instruction should allow students to use what they already know to arrive at new understandings. If learning is to be a constructive process, learners should engage in tasks that have meaning for them (that is the tasks should be situated in comprehensible contexts) and that allow what they already know to enter into new learning. (p. 237)

Scaffolding students up the ladder of guided reading levels can lead us to assume too much responsibility during guided reading despite evidence that independent learning in classrooms can happen only where there are authentic opportunities for students to engage in learning outside the direct control of teachers (Glynn, 1983). In guided reading sessions, we have found ourselves prompting almost continually. We have learned, however, that this excessive support is less scaffolding students and more carrying them.

Literacy education's arrival at the understanding that specific prompts to meaning, structure, and print (i.e., does that make sense? does that sound right? does that look right?) make us, as reading educators, feel that we are using a model of the reading process to inform our instruction. However, if we prompt so specifically and so often, rather than keeping our comments to a "minimum to maintain the forward momentum of students" (Deford et al., 1991, p. 109), we remove from students the opportunity to own the reading process. If a student pauses on a word, and we say, "Get your mouth ready," we eliminate the opportunity for that student to puzzle through the silent question, what do I do next? If we do this enough, we cause students to habituate waiting for our prompt, which can be as problematic as teaching them to wait for us to tell them the word.

Calkins (2001) writes of observing Pinnell working with guided reading groups. Pinnell prompted students by asking, "'What was the tricky part?' or 'Where did you do some good reading work?'" (Calkins, 2001, p. 177). This broad prompting results in a reflective teaching point. When we prompt a group of students broadly as they read from texts they can handle, they experience a tremendous amount of learning. If you are prompting extensively and specifically, you may need to examine the level of text in which your students work. If you are confident that the text level is appropriate for a particular group, you might engage some of the language in Table 12.

Whereas specific prompts are elegant in the way they fit the behaviors of students, and they are viable options for supporting students in shared reading or individual conferences, more general prompts require students to think more deeply about the text. As DeFord and colleagues (1991) recommend, the choice of text should support the reader without "specific item teaching" (p. 107). We suggest that you largely teach students to puzzle through specific decisions around specific prompts during shared

Table 12. Prompting During Guided Reading

Prompts That Narrow Student Thinking and Create Dependence	Prompts That Broaden Student Thinking and Develop Independence
"Sound it out."	"What do you know about this word?"
"Get your mouth ready."	"Try something."
"Does that make sense?" "Does that sound right?" "Does that look right?"	"Try that again." "Something didn't work." "Read that sentence (or word) again and find the problem."
"Look at the picture."	"How can you check?" "How do you know?" "How else do you know?"

reading contexts and keep your prompts during guided reading as few and as general as you can.

In a study of teacher actions that develop student independence, Watson (1999) describes "facilitative teacher behavior" during guided literacy work with small groups. Notice Watson's definition of the role of student independence within a guided context:

> The children did not require the teacher to constantly tell them what to do or how to carry out each task. They proceeded using their own initiative.... An expectation that children could operate independently prevailed. By continuous encouragement to build on their own strengths, and with support for their efforts, a momentum was established and maintained. One could almost say that the teachers required and expected children to engage in independent learning. (p. 68)

High levels of independence and near independence are central to guided reading sessions. You can foster this independence by thoughtfully prompting students to integrate information across a text.

Strategy #20: Consider the Efficacy of Each Student's Self-Correcting Behaviors

With the work of Goodman (1985), educators began to think of mistakes in reading as miscues or windows into students' systems for processing text and opportunities to consider the ways they integrate sources of information as they read. With the work of Clay (1991), we began to view self-correcting behaviors as a particularly valuable tool for students and evidence that they are weighing one source of information against another. There seem to be two primary views on interpreting the self-correcting behaviors of students. The first is that a mistake is a bad thing, and all errors in reading are equal. The second, more common view is that self-correcting behaviors are a universally positive sign that students are integrating the cues. This common literacy wisdom falls short when we look closely at the ways students integrate information to arrive at self-corrections.

Rather than considering self-corrections as evidence of good processing, we suggest you consider them evidence of *better* processing than uncorrected errors and generally worse processing than not making an error in the first place. Although we can consider self-correcting behaviors a positive sign, because they indicate that the student is working to engage cues from multiple sources of information, if a student adopts self-correcting as a strategy for reading in itself, then these self-correcting behaviors become inefficient. Self-correcting can become too much of a good thing.

For example, David, a second grader, has a word recognition percentage on a particular passage of 97%, which would indicate that the text is comfortably within his instructional reading level. However, he engaged in self-correcting behaviors 14 times in the assessed passage of 100 words. Even though he corrected 80% of his errors, he is not efficient in his reading process. Rather than using self-correcting as a device for repairing occasional errors on the run, he has developed a habit of not carefully attending to print and letting story alert him if he has misread a word. This excessive behavior presents as an inefficient pattern across David's reading and is masked by the high percentages he gets on accuracy. His teacher has not addressed his overdependence on story and his underutilization of print, because he consistently reads from grade-level texts within instructional-level parameters and generally understands what he reads.

This habituated, inefficient process for reading is likely to fall apart for David as he begins to encounter more concept-dense text. Furthermore, a student who corrects 80% of five errors is much more efficient than a student who corrects 80% of 20 errors. As students read increasingly difficult material in the upper elementary grades, such wasteful methods of reading and rereading will support them less and less.

If David attends more consistently to print and capitalizes on opportunities to confirm rather than negate his word recognition when he accesses story, he will move toward a more efficient reading process. He would likely benefit from an instructional strategy that supports him in breaking his inefficient processing habits, such as the next strategy.

Strategy #21: Help Students Break Inefficient Reading Habits

After much experience with students, we have found that excessive misreading is often simply a habit that students have developed to cope with repeated experiences in difficult text. When students learn to navigate frustration-level text, as defined by Betts, by relying too heavily on story or print, they develop and habituate inefficient reading processes that are likely to stay with them, even when they move back into easier reading material. All readers make mistakes, even good readers. Usually, reading with absolute accuracy involves sacrificing some other aspect of the reading task. Proficient readers do make errors; they don't, however, make very many of them. So, students who make excessive errors develop inefficient reading processes, even when their errors make sense in context or if the students correct them.

Sometimes, students who have habituated ineffective practices read words accurately in isolation and then read them inaccurately in context. That is, they read known words incorrectly during connected reading, because they have a habit of relying more on story than on print. The reading in Figure 8 demonstrates this pattern with the example that we created based on *Goldilocks and the Three Bears*. When students accurately read words like *family* but misread words like *the*, it usually does not mean that they have issues with sight words, but rather that they have difficulties with integrating print and story.

Figure 8. Difficulties With Integrated Processing

Once upon a time, a family of three bears lived in a little house in the woods.

One morning, the bear family left to walk, because their food was too hot to

eat. A girl went into their house. She found the food and ate from the bowl

that was not too hot or too cold. She sat in the best chair and broke it in two.

She tried all three bear beds and went to sleep in Baby Bear's bed. When the

three bears came home, they saw her in the little bed. She was afraid and ran

home.

Other times, these behaviors manifest in students misreading and self-correcting excessively, as we illustrate with the example in Figure 9. There are other behaviors that, when demonstrated in excess, illustrate inefficient ways of dealing with the text. For example, excessively rereading words and phrases, as illustrated in Figure 10, and not reading through the ends of the words can both indicate other difficulties with integrated processing.

To address these patterns, teachers sometimes talk to students and say something like, "Lois, I know you know all these words, because you read them all on the sight word test yesterday, but today you missed them during guided reading. You need to pay better attention to the words as you are reading." Lois, likely to be confused, probably will not correct this unconscious behavior on her own even if she tries. Her habit is as well established as any other habit, such as cracking knuckles or biting fingernails. Few people can stop these unconscious behaviors just because someone points out that they need to do so. Failure to change the

Figure 9. Inefficient Self-Correcting Behaviors

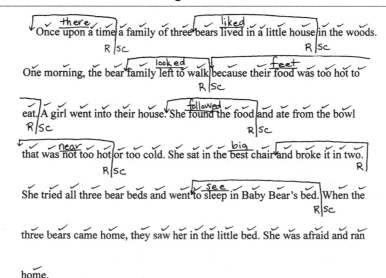

Figure 10. Other Difficulties With Integrated Processing

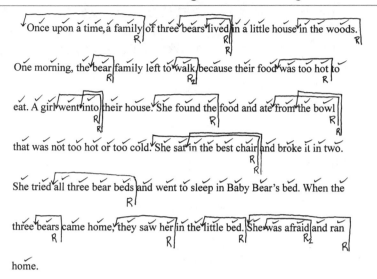

behavior after the teacher has explained the need to pay better attention while reading sometimes leads the teacher to believe that students are intentionally ignoring their instructions or that students are "lazy" readers. Neither is likely to be the case.

For students who need to break a habit, a teacher can draw their attention to the habit during the reading. A teacher might work with the student individually or pair the student with a partner or tutor for a game of "uh-oh/you did it!" If the student reads a sentence without engaging in the bad habit, then the partner says "You did it!" and the reader gets a point. If the student repeats, leaves off the end of the word, or engages in whatever habit you are trying to break, then the partner says "Uh-oh" at the end of the sentence, and the student gets an "uh-oh" point. The object of the game is for the reader to get more "you did it!" points than "uh-oh" points.

During her work with struggling readers, Jan has seen students begin to rearrange their reading processes with only one session of playing this game. The beauty of "uh-oh/you did it!" is that it works with a student's intact reading process rather than breaking it into isolated parts. Students tend to find this game empowering, because they do the work and see significant progress in a relatively short time. For these students, their compromised process is limiting their progress. Once habits are broken, readers tend to make tremendous, rapid growth as they engage a solid, integrated process.

This game is not practical during guided reading, since it is a one-on-one activity to set students up for success in guided reading. Balancing students' reading processes in this way sets them up for long-term progress as readers. If they have solid, balanced reading processes, students read increasingly difficult texts with understanding. Otherwise, as text difficulty increases, they tend to engage the support of the inefficient habit even more, and progress slows.

You can modify this game by letting students record themselves reading. Then, they listen to the tape while they follow along with the text and simply tally the number of sentences they read without engaging in the bad habit. Usually, if students listen to a tape recording of their reading and compare it to the text, they notice their mistakes.

We have also used running records to support this work. We make running records of students' readings and then reread them to the students, exactly as they originally read them, while they follow along. Students are startled to see the ways they make the reading process inefficient for themselves. We say to them something like, "I am going to read this story back to you just the way you read it, and I want you to tell me what you notice." Most students discover for themselves their patterns of inaccuracy.

Then, we talk with them about specific words with which they were inaccurate, words that they may know in isolation. We write down a word they missed during the reading, such as *this*, and ask a student to read it in isolation. When the student reads it correctly, we say, "You said this word was *its* when you just read." The students are usually surprised. We tell them that they have many strengths in reading and a few little things that are getting in their way. We tell them that we are going to show them how to break some habits, that this work will make them even stronger readers, and that we are going to help them.

This game is valuable for students who excessively repeat words or phrases, self-correct, or make print errors that make contextual and structural sense. We want to stress the word *excessively* here, as repetitions, self-corrections, and contextually reasonable print errors represent healthy reading when they appear in limited ways. As is often the case, when the behaviors are extreme, they tend to indicate a pattern that is likely to impede the progress of the student.

Strategy #22: Provide Massive Practice

The highest level of work on integrating processing is engaging in interactions with connected text. The more students actually read complete sentences across complete texts, the more we help them solidify efficient integrated processing of cues from different information sources. This massive practice presents two challenges: First, we have to give students more time to read. With more and more to teach as standards-based curricula drive the efforts of teachers and students, it sometimes feels like increasing students' time reading from connected texts is time stolen from "real" instruction. Without time to practice the strategies and skills we have taught, however, students are unlikely to habituate the behaviors that make them look, sound, and understand as proficient readers do.

We are not saying that you should add an extra hour of silent reading to your instructional day. Rather, mine your schedule for minutes and look for the accumulation of reading opportunities these minutes might offer. For example, if you use centers during literacy instruction, listening to appropriately paced stories on tape or CD is more valuable than students making their names with magnetic letters. Rewriting patterned stories from guided reading texts is generally more beneficial than practicing writing the letter P in isolation. Whenever possible, give students opportunities to engage in authentic literacy practice.

The second challenge associated with giving students massive reading practice is that this practice must be from texts that are appropriate for the students in terms of level. By *appropriate*, we mean that they are quantitatively and qualitatively suitable given a particular instructional context. The students should read accurately, deeply, and fluently (i.e., quantitative indicators) and enjoy the reading, demonstrate success, and be relatively free from stress (i.e., qualitative indicators).

Of course, the difficulty of the text will vary across the gradual release of responsibility. We will not always be exact in matching students to texts, and we sometimes have to compromise our efforts to meet individual needs as we consider a group. Nevertheless, one of our highest priorities as teachers of literacy is to give students as much practice as possible from texts that support their self-extending systems for integrating information.

Putting It All Together

Teaching students toward integrated processing involves showing them the ways that a text supports a reader with redundant sources of information. Teaching students to compare and contrast cues from multiple sources of information fosters reader independence and sets in place a system that helps the students teach themselves. We become better at fostering student independence as we constantly consider the ways we take on work that students should do themselves.

All readers make mistakes, a reality that preserves our comprehension and fluency. That is, if we corrected every mistake we made, even those that do not compromise the meaning of the text, we would sacrifice fluency and comprehension.

Certain errors and patterns of error, however, represent better processing on the part of the reader than others. All errors are not equal. Even acceptable errors that accumulate can pose a threat to later, or even current, reading progress. If these inefficient behaviors present as patterns, teach proactively to help students break these reading habits that do not serve them. Most important, let students read a lot more. Practice makes permanent, so let them practice from texts that allow them to successfully engage their natural tendencies toward repair.

QUESTIONS FOR REFLECTION AND CONVERSATION

1. How and when are you teaching students to engage in integrated processing of text information?

2. When are acceptable errors acceptable, and when are they problematic?

3. Think of particular students who have demonstrated excess with acceptable errors. How did they negotiate the demands of connected text? How will you help them?

4. How can your prompting during guided reading better support students in integrated processing?

5. How will you increase your students' opportunities to engage with connected text?

6. With what in this chapter do you agree? Why? With what in this chapter do you disagree? Why?

A Literacy Story: Mr. Jenkins Administers Literacy Assessments

It is August, and Mr. Jenkins, as he always does, administers a benchmark assessment with each student in his new second-grade class. The assessment involves a series of small books that are leveled A–Z, exactly the way the books he uses for guided reading are leveled. He begins a level or two below the reported reading level for the students at the end of the previous year and continues until he locates each student's ceiling, or the point at which the students move beyond instructional-level parameters for word recognition, comprehension, and fluency.

Mr. Jenkins makes a record of students' readings by using a running record form that has the words of the text already printed on it. The form is a traditional running record in the sense that there is designated space for analyzing the meaning, structural, and visual cues students use as well as the self-correcting behaviors they exhibit.

Because each of his 22 students reads from several texts at a number of levels, Mr. Jenkins only has time to actually analyze the running records that he has determined to be instructional level for the students. He staples these to each student's stack of assessment papers, so the instructional-level reading record is on top. He is able to see at a glance, simply by looking at the analysis, if students are using visual, meaning, or structural cues. His focus, however, is on assigning the students to groups for guided reading, and he takes the packets of assessment materials for each student and sorts them into stacks based on the highest word recognition level of each student.

CHAPTER 6

Redesigning Literacy Assessment

When my friend Lessie runs she runs so fast
I can hardly see her feet touch the ground
She runs faster than a leaf flies...

From "Lessie" in *Honey, I Love and Other Love Poems* by Eloise Greenfield

We can, in our minds, quantify Lessie's running, mark it with a stopwatch, and chart her progress with graphs, but we learn the truth of Lessie as a runner when we listen to someone who watches her carefully and offers us insightful descriptions of the way Lessie "pushes her knees up and down" and "opens her mouth and tastes the wind" as "her coat flies out behind her" (Greenfield, 1972, p. 14). These qualitative offerings tell us the story of Lessie the runner, just as our listening to students read can tell us their stories of literacy.

Mr. Jenkins's practice of listening to students read from texts that are from the floor to the ceiling of their reading abilities gives him a wealth of information about his students and puts him in good stead to design instruction specific to their needs. Fortunately, guided reading is not a program, and many school districts that have adopted guided reading have supported this adoption with generous opportunities for professional learning. In many cases, this professional learning is job embedded, ongoing, and thoughtfully designed. We are arguably at a point in history when teachers have deeper conceptual understandings of literacy instruction and more mindful methods for letting these understandings shape their practice than ever before.

Still, the rush of the classroom and the pressure to have students "on grade level" can force us to make compromises. One of these compromises tends to be in the area of analyzing the reading behaviors of students. Generally, if we keep running records, we feel as if we are ahead, and truly we are. We invest in a false economy, however, when we shortchange the analysis of reading behaviors, because the understandings we gather from these can actually help us meet the goals we are under such pressure to reach.

At present, it seems most of us predominantly use running records, benchmarks, or informal reading inventories to determine or verify student placement in a particular level of text. Even when we analyze reading behaviors, in terms of the daily use of running records, unless a student's word recognition on a particular text is below 90%, we may not pay attention to the reading process of the student. And although our understandings of literacy may be deeper than ever, they generally don't support thinking of these assessments beyond numerical summaries. Clay (2002) has likened distilling a student's reading process down to a few quantitative indicators to using the final score of a football game to evaluate the performance of the players in an effort to help them improve their game. Word recognition percentages and other scores, even ratios of self-corrections, don't give us a complete picture of how a student interacted with the text and integrated various cueing systems.

Clarifying Differences in Common Literacy Assessments

The labels for various common literacy assessments have evolved and meshed. Generally, this evolution is evidence of improvement, as we have made our tools fit our work. There is, nonetheless, residual confusion, simply because original labels, such as *running record*, don't necessarily match original designs or intents. For purposes of clarity in this chapter, we want to establish some general definitions of common literacy assessments, as you bring to this text your experiences with how each assessment has evolved in your instructional context.

Informal Reading Inventories (IRIs)

IRIs are more formal than formative and involve some standardization in administration. IRIs include detailed documentation that accurately represents the student's reading and begin with a text that is relatively easy for a student (i.e., a basal level). Then, teachers give students increasingly difficult texts until the texts get too hard (i.e., the students reach their ceiling). The texts for IRIs are usually all within a single book, with a few paragraphs or pages dedicated to each individual level, or a series of pages copied from a manual. These stories generally include comprehension questions specific to each level of text, and many include assessment considerations for analyzing student retelling of the text.

IRIs include directions for analyzing the errors of students and are usually normed based on field testing. The codes for marking errors in IRIs may vary across assessments, although the types of errors are generally consistent. The forms for analyzing IRIs usually differ considerably from the analysis in a running record, although most consider the ways that students access sources of information.

Running Records

Running records, created by Clay, were designed to be formative assessment tools. Although running records, like IRIs, record student oral reading in its entirety, one prominent distinguishing factor between running records and IRIs is that teachers complete running records on a running record form or blank sheet of paper that does not have the words of the text on it. This feature of running records is at the heart of their purpose, that is, Clay developed these as a tool for busy teachers to administer on the run. She writes, "Teachers should learn to take running records in ways that will allow them to use this technique—with any child on any text, at any time" (Clay, 2000, p. 7).

In terms of assessing story, running records do not include quantitative considerations of fluency or comprehension. With each error, teachers analyze whether students consider meaning (i.e., story) on a sentence level, but there are no comprehension questions, since the tool is not specific to particular texts. Teachers often make notes, however, about how students integrate information while they are reading, which may include references to use of story information.

Clay speaks strongly about the limitations of using a preprinted text to document student reading, saying that using these texts is something to avoid. So, any written record of student reading in which the teacher makes notes on a preprinted copy of the text is, by definition, not a running record. Although running records are relatively accurate records of a student's readings from particular texts, and they note the same patterns of reading recorded in IRIs, they are less formal than IRIs and should be an automatic form of record keeping for teachers that they can use daily. We generally recommend that teachers record one running record per day for one student. This procedure usually means that teachers have at least one running record per student each month.

Splitting the Difference With Benchmarking Kits

Here is where the conversation gets complicated; it is easy to see how we have grown confused by these assessment semantics. Many schools have purchased commercial benchmarking kits that include a set of graded, little books that are leveled in the same ways that Reading Recovery or guided reading books are leveled. The assessments are more formal and document student reading from basal to ceiling, so they are basically IRIs. The forms, however, for analyzing these assessments often replicate Clay's running records.

Benchmark assessments often call these records of reading *running records*, even though that term is technically inaccurate, because the forms generally have the entire text on them. These assessments also have various comprehension measures, such as questions or retelling options, for evaluating student use of story information. The analysis elements for benchmarking kits may vary, although most recently they tend to mirror the analysis procedures Clay developed for running records.

Benchmarking systems resemble IRIs in their formality, continua of text difficulty, and use of forms that include a copy of the text. These systems may relate to running records in their analysis and, perhaps, in their use of small books. Benchmarking systems vary in terms of how extensively they are normed or field tested before they are marketed, so they do not all have high levels of validity or reliability. All three of these assessments—IRIs, running records, and benchmarking systems—aim to document the ways students process information *during* reading. To call the documentation of the texts within benchmarking systems running records, however, is counter to Clay's original intent. Running records are documentations of authentic readings, thus more formative, whereas IRIs and benchmark assessments are documentations of reading in a testing situation, more summative. Figure 11 compares running records, IRIs, and benchmark assessments.

Figure 11. Comparison of Literacy Assessments

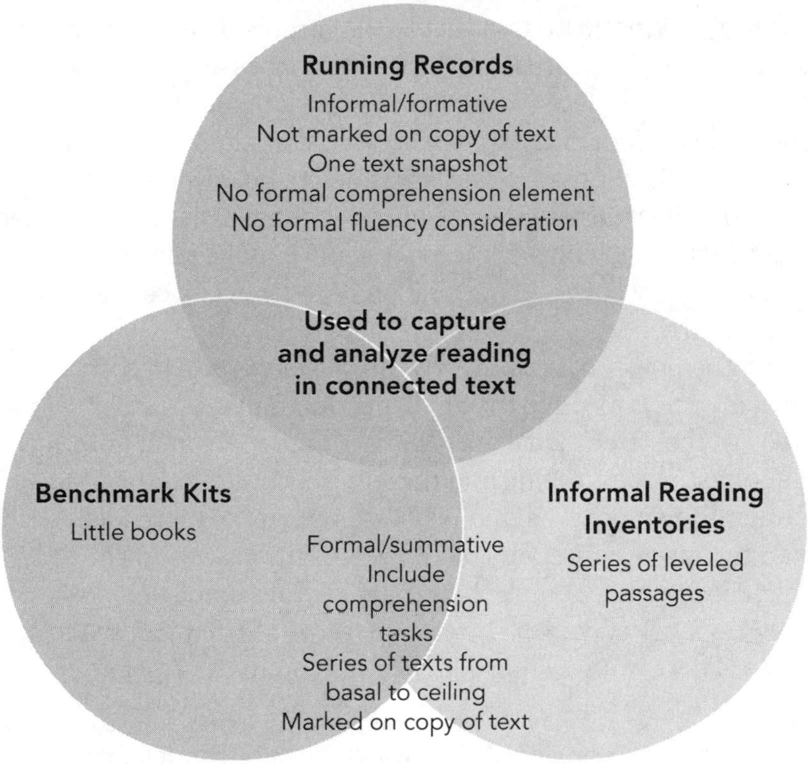

Running Records
Informal/formative
Not marked on copy of text
One text snapshot
No formal comprehension element
No formal fluency consideration

**Used to capture
and analyze reading
in connected text**

Benchmark Kits
Little books

Formal/summative
Include
comprehension
tasks
Series of texts from
basal to ceiling
Marked on copy of text

**Informal Reading
Inventories**
Series of leveled
passages

Again, the differences in these assessments are often a matter of semantics; if you have been referring to benchmark assessments as running records, it is probably because the authors of the assessments do, too. Furthermore, it doesn't really matter, as long as you are considering both formative and summative opportunities to document student reading. Nevertheless, for purposes of discussion in this chapter, we needed some clarity of language. Our use of the term *IRI* refers to the uses of graded texts from basal to ceiling, both within reading inventories and sets of benchmark texts. When we speak of *running records*, we are referring to the daily, on-the-run, formative assessments designed by Clay to capture authentic reading of any text.

Using Assessments to Understand Student Reading Processes

As the opening vignette for this chapter illustrates, IRIs are commonly used to make grouping decisions. Running records are often used to verify these grouping decisions or to see if a particular text presented instructional-level demands for a particular student. These uses are viable and practical applications of these assessments; however, in this chapter, we suggest that it is worthwhile to examine the assessments more deeply. The insight that these tools offer into students' balanced negotiations with print and story cues and integrations of these cues can give teachers instructional direction.

We find the power of learning to administer running records (and IRIs) invaluable to informing instructional decisions, and we offer some expansions of their traditional analysis. In the sections that follow, we present suggestions for optimizing these important assessment tools for documenting student reading processes. Many of these ideas are supported by our modified version of the running record form. We include in Figure 12 a complete sample, based on our version of *Goldilocks and the Three Bears* below, which you can reference throughout the following discussions. There is also a reproducible version in the Appendix.

> Once upon a time, a family of three bears lived in a little house in the woods. One morning, the bear family left to walk, because their food was too hot to eat. A girl went into their house. She found the food and ate from the bowl that was not too hot or too cold. She sat in the best chair and broke it in two. She tried all three bear beds and went to sleep in Baby Bear's bed. When the three bears came home, they saw her in the little bed. She was afraid and ran home.

Working Through the Tricky Parts

Strategy #23: Move Beyond the All-or-None Systems

Traditionally, error analysis of the visual system, or print, in IRIs has involved thoughtful examinations of student use of the elements of print. As running records don't typically include such detailed analysis, considerations are simply around whether a student is using visual (i.e., print) information. Similar limitations are present in considerations of

Figure 12. Sample Alternate Running Record Form

Student: James Doe   **Date:** 10-1-09   **Recorder:** Melody Croft

Word Recognition Accuracy: __97__ % Comprehension (1–5): __4__ Fluency (1–4): __3__
Total Errors: __5__   Self-Corrections: __2__   % Self-Corrected: 40%
Independent: _____ Instructional: ___✓___ Frustration: _____

How efficiently does the student...   Notes

		Notes
use print?	0 1 2 ③ 4 5	Has many print skills, but is not looking at the whole word. Commonly overlooks middles and endings of words.
use story?	0 1 2 ③ 4 5	Generally understands. Substituted "angry" for "afraid," which indicates subtle misunderstandings.
integrate cues?	0 1 ② 3 4 5	Not efficiently using structure to cross-check. Needs to self-correct.

Running Record and Error Analysis   Print   Story

Page	Title: "Goldilocks and the Three Bears"	Level:	Running Words: 100	Beginning	Middle	End	Meaning	Structure	Self-Corrections
	✓✓✓✓ ✓✓✓✓✓✓✓ h– / ho– / ✓✓✓. house			✓	✓		✓	✓	
	✓✓✓ ✓ ✓✓ want |R| sc ✓✓✓✓ ✓✓ walk			✓	✓				✓
	✓✓✓✓✓✓✓ fi– |finded ✓✓✓✓✓✓ big |R| sc found bowl			✓ ✓		✓ ✓	✓ ✓	✓	✓
	✓✓✓ ✓✓✓✓. ✓✓✓✓✓✓ broked ✓✓. broke			✓	✓		✓		
	✓✓✓✓✓✓✓✓✓✓✓. ✓✓								
	✓✓✓ ✓✓✓✓✓✓ ✓✓. ✓✓ angry ✓✓ afraid			✓				✓	
	✓.								
			Totals	6/6	3/6	2/6	4/6	3/6	2/6
			Percentages	100	50	33	66	50	33

story, as meaning and structure are analyzed in the same all-or-none fashion.

Consider the following summary of Grace's reading:

Grace is a second-grade student who read a Level K text with 86% accuracy before self-corrections and 95% accuracy considering self-correcting behaviors. Grace, with almost all of her errors, considers print, as there is beginning graphic similarity between most of her errors and the text. That is, when she makes an error, it is usually with the letters in the middle or at the end of the words. In terms of story, all of her errors make sense and sound right in sentence-level context, so she is consistently using the meaning and structural systems. Furthermore, she engages in self-correcting behaviors most of the time, which is why her word recognition percentage is so high.

At a glance, one might draw the conclusion from looking at Grace's running record that she is a balanced, proficient reader, as she is integrating cues and cross-checking them against each other. To this appraisal, we would respond, why then is she making so many errors in the first place? We are inclined to look at how *well* she uses print and story rather than simply whether she uses them at all. Grace does have some skill in accessing and integrating cues; however, she does not have *enough* skill for us to describe her as proficient in the assessed text. She is not exhibiting a smoothly operating system.

Specifically, she is using the initial, and sometimes the final, print cues. Although one can accurately circle the *V* for *visual* under analysis on her running record, indicating that she is using the visual cues (i.e., print), this is an all-or-none proposition, and the analysis does not really allow for closer consideration of just how well Grace uses print.

As this example illustrates, interpretations of student use of visual cues can vary greatly. For example, a student who says *me* for *at* may be using visual information. Certainly, there is graphic similarity of note that the student may have accessed, since the student did not say *hippopotamus*. We would question, however, the efficiency of this student's use of print. Similarly, third graders who still look at the first letter and guess based on context will be described by a running record (and many IRIs at present) as using visual cues, whereas we maintain that third graders should be more efficient as they utilize print.

Toward the end of looking more specifically at the print elements that students do and do not use, some Reading Recovery teachers have adapted their notations on their running records by writing V_B, V_M, and V_E. Looking at graphic similarity at the beginning, middle, and end of the word gives teachers specific information about exactly how much of the print the student is attending to. This analysis mirrors the traditional analysis in IRIs, and we think it incredibly worthwhile. We find, however, the process of writing V_B, V_M, and V_E with each error tedious. Instead, we offer an alternative format for analyzing student reading behaviors, using a set of columns and checks rather than asking teachers to write out codes for each error.

Two procedures for looking at story help us understand student reading processes related to how *well* they understand the story. First, like Clay, we analyze use of meaning, or context, and use of language structure. So, a student who reads "I like to fish" when the text is "I like fish" is using the context and the structure of the text in ways that are related to each other. Rather than write *M* for meaning and *S* for structure, as is customary, we carry the columns that support the analysis of print into our analysis of story by providing a column for checking off attention to meaning and structure. In addition, we analyze story even further through the use of the comprehension continuum we describe next.

Strategy #24: Analyze Comprehension Holistically

When scoring an IRI, the comprehension questions or the retellings are often used to absolutely quantify whether students comprehend the text. For example, if a student correctly answers three out of four questions, he or she comprehends the text at 75% accuracy, and most reading teachers will, understandably, consider this a passing score in comprehension. There aren't usually considerations of partially correct answers, questions that are poorly worded, or the ways other indicators may demonstrate comprehension. Teachers express frustrations with these limitations. Usually, the questions require more explicit than implicit responses, so students who don't consistently make the necessary inferences often still pass the comprehension requirements of the assessment. As for retellings, the measures of these are often detail heavy, again neglecting the deeper elements of the text. These assessments seem to offer little opportunity to really quantify the depth of student comprehension.

To address these challenges, we recommend that you consider comprehension holistically along the following continuum. This continuum of understanding of story describes just how well a student comprehends the text (see Table 13). At first glance, the scale may seem limited, but all our efforts to make it more specific have complicated it unnecessarily and compromised its reliability. Inevitably, we return to this original design for the consistency it offers and the ease with which we can use it. We use the continuum to holistically consider all the indications that a student comprehends the text.

Quite simply, in using the continuum, the teacher considers all the ways that students demonstrate a grasp of story during the reading. During an IRI or running record, this consideration may include errors that make sense semantically or syntactically, use of self-corrections based on context or language structure, fluency, inflection, attention to punctuation, spontaneous comments about the story, answers to factual questions, answers to inferential questions, facial expressions, story retellings, and anything else that gives us insight into the student's grasp of the text. Basically, teachers consider all the ways students demonstrate a grasp of story and evaluate them holistically on a scale of 1 to 5, with 1 representing little or no understanding and 5 representing deep, profound understanding that taps into the themes, subtleties, or big ideas of the text.

To further explain the comprehension continuum, we offer Table 14, which presents retellings of *Little Red Riding Hood*. It does not imply that a student's level of comprehension along the previous rubric is gauged exclusively by a retelling. Rather, the depth of comprehension

Table 13. Comprehension Continuum

1	The student did not understand the story.
2	The student misunderstood much of the story.
3	The student had some confusion about and some understanding of the story.
4	The student understood the story.
5	The student deeply understood the story.

Table 14. Illustrative Retellings of *Little Red Riding Hood*

1	The girl wore a red dress to a party.
2	The girl wore a red cape and took some food to a party. Her grandmother was there.
3	The girl wore a red cape and took some food to her sick grandmother. Her grandmother dressed up like a wolf to scare her.
4	The girl wore a red cape and took some food to her grandmother. On the way, the girl met a wolf who later ate her grandmother, and so forth.
5	The girl wore a red cape and took some food to her grandmother. On the way, she met a wolf who later ate her grandmother, and so forth. The girl learned a lesson about heeding her mother's instructions.

represented in the retellings represents the depth of comprehension that a student might demonstrate in a number of ways, all of which a teacher would consider within a single passage, text, or level of an IRI or running record. Jan has used the comprehension continuum with groups of teachers extensively. It has demonstrably high inter-rater reliability that we can quantify informally simply by saying that roughly four out of five teachers will place a student on the same point on this continuum. The opinion that varies will only differ by one point. Never in Jan's extensive work with this continuum have teachers differed from each other by more than one point.

Because this continuum is so simple, the 1–5 scale can become part of a teacher's vocabulary around students' reading processes. Many teachers write a number between 1 and 5 for comprehension at the top of each running record to give comprehension a formal place in these assessments. This rubric also informs our general conversations about student reading, even if we are not talking about assessment. We might ask, how well did the student understand the text? when we are reflecting on a guided reading lesson or a read-aloud. This question is relevant in many contexts beyond our administrations of literacy assessments.

Strategy #25: Use Fluency to Help Determine Instructional Reading Level

Fluency is the third variable that we recommend you always consider when examining student reading processes, whether in assessments or simply in observations during a guided reading lesson. This dimension of reading is easy to grasp on a conceptual level. Few people would argue against fluency; it would be a bit like arguing against peace. In terms of classroom practicalities, however, fluency is often that last piece of the reading process puzzle that we manage to explain away. We say things like, "He isn't fluent, but that's the way he talks," or "My students who are struggling the most are actually on grade level. They aren't really fluent, but they can figure out the words and they generally understand the stories."

Like the comprehension scores described in the previous section, we like to include fluency measures in the daily running records we administer; we think it is that important. Practice makes permanent, and students who practice reading without fluency establish a paradigm for a fractured process. If you want students to be stronger, independent readers, consider fluency in your assessments and support the students in reading fluently during shared, guided, and independent reading.

For ease of discussion, we use a very general application of the Fountas and Pinnell (1996) fluency rubric, which is on a scale of 1–4:

1 = The student is reading almost all word by word.

2 = The student is reading mostly word by word, but sometimes sounds like a strong reader.

3 = The student mostly sounds like a strong reader, but sometimes reads word by word.

4 = The student sounds like a strong reader.

When Jan explains this rubric to teachers, she actually tells them that Level 5, which is only implied, means that a student has read with perfect fluency. She goes on to explain that even strong readers don't read perfectly, because to do so would compromise other elements of the reading process. So, the fifth level in the fluency rubric is theoretical rather than practical. However, this imaginary Level 5 supports our understandings and helps us align the comprehension continuum with the fluency rubric.

Like the comprehension continuum, we appreciate the simplicity of this tool. It does not dissect fluency in terms of repetitions, punctuation, sound-outs, and so forth. This simplicity does not mean, however, that we can't think about specific reading patterns related to fluency—we certainly do. It just means that we begin our appraisals of student fluency with the big picture in mind.

Again, reliability is easy to achieve with this measure. In working with teachers, Jan has been able to support them in reaching a high level of consistency in one-time, professional learning experiences. Furthermore, this consistency of rating becomes consistency of thought about the ways students process text aloud. The 1–4 scale gives us a common paradigm of a smoothly operating reading process and a common vocabulary that facilitates our conversations about how we can better teach our students.

Strategy #26: Consider the Ways Students Integrate Cues

We describe students who efficiently integrate cues from print and story as balanced. We recognize the limitations of this description; certainly it is overused in the literature. We do, however, appreciate the opportunities for conversation and the focus on process that the term *balance* affords. Quite simply, it is not a perfect descriptor, but it has worked for us in profound ways and offers us a common vocabulary. Please apply, explore, and adapt it as you find useful. The point is not the word *balance*, but the ways that students are integrating information.

Although the culminating event for most IRIs and running records is the final calculating that tells a teacher whether the assessed text is on the reader's instructional reading level, for us the heart of the assessment is to evaluate integration within the student's reading process. We are interested less in tallying errors and more in thinking about students' whole reading processes. To support our conversations, we use a scale that illustrates whether students use print more than story, or vice versa, and to what degree. This scale is at the top of our running record form (see Figure 12 earlier in this chapter and the reproducible in the Appendix) and is, for us, the most important aspect of the assessment.

To a student such as Jasmine, presented in Chapter 4, who consistently only uses print and doesn't even access the story support in the form of pictures prominent on the page, we would assign a 5 on the print portion of the scale and a 0 on the story and integration scales (see Figure 13). A student who persistently makes errors that are completely dissimilar graphically but make sense in terms of story receives a 5 on the story side of the scale. Like the comprehension continuum and the fluency rubric, this scale is a holistic measure. How does a student's reading process

Figure 13. Analysis of the Reading Process for a Print-Dependent Reader

How efficiently does the student...		Notes
use print?	0 1 2 3 (4) 5	Automatically decodes when problem-solving. Some difficulty with vowels.
use story?	0 (1) 2 3 4 5	Does not seem to use context or structure much. Sometimes offers phonetically plausible nonsense word.
integrate cues?	0 (1) 2 3 4 5	Not monitoring. Does not stop when reading; does not make sense even when there is strong story support in the text.

Figure 14. Analysis of the Reading Process for a Story-Dependent Reader

How efficiently does the student...		Notes
use print?	0 1 (2) 3 4 5	Mostly looks at first letter and guesses based on story.
use story?	0 1 2 (3) 4 5	Relies heavily on story but works on a sentence level. Errors often make sense within a sentence but don't work across the whole story.
integrate cues?	0 1 2 (3) 4 5	Some monitoring, but if error makes sense on any level, will not correct.

generally look? For example, a student who usually makes errors such as *puppy* instead of *dog* is scored to indicate an inefficient dependence on story at the expense of print, as in Figure 14.

Students who sound like proficient readers, who demonstrate a smoothly operating system through their efficient processing of the text, receive a 4 or 5 in each area, which indicates that they are ably integrating aspects of print and story. Again, the term *balance* is limited, as students will not neatly access print exactly as many times as story or always confirm one against the other. In general, however, these students have competence in both of these areas and use them to confirm and cross-check.

This evaluation is very subjective and, as there are 11 scoring options, groups of teachers are less consistent in gauging this than with the fluency and comprehension rubrics. We assert, however, that absolute consistency is less critical for this evaluation than general consistency, and teachers are almost without fail in the neighborhood of each other with this scale. Furthermore, the discussions that ensue as teachers explain their thinking behind their score determinations are more valuable than the scores themselves. Jan has found that engaging teachers in these kinds of discussions has resulted in dramatically shifting paradigms from focusing on level to focusing on reading process.

In alignment with our discussions from previous chapters, our assignment to guided reading groups is based on our determinations of the highest level at which a student is balanced. Although they are still important, we place less emphasis on isolated numbers, such as percentage of words read correctly, self-correction ratios, and percentage of comprehension questions answered correctly, and more emphasis on them in combination, because they inform our thinking about how a student integrates information during reading. Furthermore, we think about student balance in this way whether we are administering an IRI, a running record, or simply listening to a student read.

Strategy #27: Look at Shifts in Students' Reading Processes Across Texts

When interpreting an IRI, after looking deeply at a student's reading process, consider the ways that it changes across levels. To help us, we have developed a Student Placement Thought Sheet (see the Appendix). By recording the word recognition, comprehension, and fluency scores on each level of text, we can see patterns. We look for the ways that a student's reading process changes in response to increasingly difficult text.

Consider Desmond's scores in Table 15. The table illustrates the ways his word recognition, comprehension, and fluency vary as the text increases in difficulty. Although common wisdom suggests that we teach Desmond from a Level E text, we argue that the 90% accuracy presents too many errors. Furthermore, at Level E, every aspect of Desmond's reading process begins to waiver. Level E is a breaking point for his word recognition, comprehension, and fluency. If nothing in terms of word recognition, comprehension, and fluency is absolutely solid, then readers are forced to cobble together their reading processes.

Table 15. Desmond's Reading Across Texts

Text Level	Word Recognition (%)	Comprehension (1–5)	Fluency (1–4)
C	100	5	4
D	98	5	4
E	90	4	3
F	87	4	2

We are also keenly aware that Level E is a critical point in terms of the text gradient. So, we are adamant about holding out for Desmond to develop a more smoothly operating process before he works from Level E texts. We know from experience that Desmond can establish a balanced reading process while working in Level D texts because of his high level of success rather than despite it. As Clay (1993) admonishes, "Cautiously increase the text difficulty," giving "massive practice" before increasing text level (p. 15).

Putting It All Together

Assessment in reading is simultaneously complicated and simple. We have tried to set in place for our students tools that help us look knowledgeably at their reading processes and subprocesses. We have also tried to organize a vocabulary that simplifies the discussions of complicated student reading behaviors and affords us opportunities to consider student learning without getting tangled in semantics. We hope this chapter recasts reading assessment for you in ways that offer new insight into the learning of your students, ways of watching as they "run," like "Lessie," with their metaphorical coats flying behind them. At the close of *Preventing Misguided Reading*, we present a big picture developed through thoughtful examinations and documentations of student reading processes. By putting it all together in assessment conversations, we hope to share insight that can inform all your literacy interactions with students.

QUESTIONS FOR REFLECTION
AND CONVERSATION

1. What formal and informal literacy assessments do you use and why? How do they support each other?

2. How does your reading assessment capture the complete reading processes of your students?

3. What are the relationships between word recognition, comprehension, and fluency in the reading assessments you administer?

4. How do you consider how *well* students use print and story when they read?

5. How does your language around assessment carry over into your language around student learning across the gradual release of responsibility?

6. With what do you agree in this chapter? Why? With what do you disagree? Why?

EPILOGUE

I f it is true that a person's cells are continually reborn and that we are all completely new every seven years, then we have lived several lifetimes in thinking about and writing this book. We understand that the ideas here are not permanent upon publication; rather, they are reborn with every reader as he or she brings to the text individual experiences and backgrounds. Perhaps you have read this book and find yourself revising the ways you think about print. Or, maybe you are rearranging your framework for considering the role of meaning making in learning to read. We did not intend this book to do specifically one or the other; we simply intended it to support the thinking relevant to you, particularly in consideration of the ways print and meaning work together. Our aim has been for our conversations to mirror the balance we seek to support in student reading processes.

We hope that you have taken from *Preventing Misguided Reading* the ideas you need to support your students in becoming literate, whether it be shifting your focus from whole to details and back again, or pulling away from detail for the sake of putting it all together and making meaning. This book continues to change, taking on new skin, every time someone reads or talks about it. And even in the margin between us putting these words on the page and you reading them, the perpetual rebirth and revision of thought that is the trademark of all reflective educators will continue its forward progression.

Reproducibles

- Alternate Running Record Form
- Student Placement Thought Sheet

ALTERNATE RUNNING RECORD FORM

Student: _____ Date: _____ Recorder: _____

Word Recognition Accuracy: _____ % Comprehension (1–5): _____ Fluency (1–4): _____
Total Errors: _____ Self-Corrections: _____ % Self-Corrected: _____
Independent: _____ Instructional: _____ Frustration: _____

How efficiently does the student...   Notes

use print?	0	1	2	3	4	5	
use story?	0	1	2	3	4	5	
integrate cues?	0	1	2	3	4	5	

Running Record and Error Analysis   Print   Story

Page	Title:	Level:	Running Words:	Beginning	Middle	End	Meaning	Structure	Self-Corrections
			Totals						
			Percentages						

(continued)

ALTERNATE RUNNING RECORD FORM (*continued*)

Student: _____ Date: _____ Recorder: _____

Running Record and Error Analysis

				Print			Story		
Page	Title:	Level:	Running Words:	Beginning	Middle	End	Meaning	Structure	Self-Corrections
			Totals						
			Percentages						

STUDENT PLACEMENT THOUGHT SHEET

Student: _____ Date: _____ Teacher: _____

Title	Text Level	Word Recognition (%)	Comprehension (1–5)	Fluency (1–4)	Notes

Preventing Misguided Reading: New Strategies for Guided Reading Teachers by Jan Miller Burkins and Melody M. Croft.
© 2010 International Reading Association. May be copied for classroom use.

REFERENCES

Adams, M.J. (1990). *Beginning to read: Thinking and learning about print.* Cambridge, MA: MIT Press.

Adams, M.J. (2004). Modeling the connections between word recognition and reading. In R.B. Ruddell & N.J. Unrau (Eds.), *Theoretical models and processes of reading* (5th ed., pp. 1219–1243). Newark, DE: International Reading Association.

Afflerbach, P., Pearson, P.D., & Paris, S.G. (2008). Clarifying differences between reading skills and reading strategies. *The Reading Teacher, 61*(5), 364–373. doi:10.1598/RT.61.5.1

Allington, R.L. (2002). You can't learn much from books you can't read. *Educational Leadership, 60*(3), 16–19.

Allington, R.L. (2006). *What really matters for struggling readers: Designing research-based programs* (2nd ed.). Boston: Allyn & Bacon.

Anderson, R.C. (2004). Role of the reader's schema in comprehension, learning, and memory. In R.B. Ruddell & N.J. Unrau (Eds.), *Theoretical models and processes of reading* (5th ed., pp. 594–606). Newark, DE: International Reading Association.

Applegate, M.D., Applegate, A.J., & Modla, V.B. (2009). "She's my best reader; she just can't comprehend": Studying the relationship between fluency and comprehension. *The Reading Teacher, 62*(6), 512–521.

Betts, E.A. (1946). *Foundations of reading instruction: With emphasis on differentiated guidance.* New York: American Book.

Boushey, G., & Moser, J. (2006). *The daily 5: Fostering literacy independence in the elementary grades.* Portland, ME: Stenhouse.

Boushey, G., & Moser, J. (2009). *The CAFE book: Engaging all students in daily literacy assessment and instruction.* Portland, ME: Stenhouse.

Brown, R., Pressley, M., Van Meter, P., & Schuder, T. (1996). A quasi-experimental validation of transactional strategies instruction with low-achieving second-grade readers. *Journal of Educational Psychology, 88*(1), 18–37. doi:10.1037/0022-0663.88.1.18

Calkins, L.M. (2001). *The art of teaching reading.* New York: Longman.

Christensen, L. (2000). *Reading, writing, and rising up: Teaching about social justice and the power of the written word.* Milwaukee, WI: Rethinking Schools.

Clay, M.M. (1979). *The early detection of reading difficulties: A diagnostic survey with recovery procedures* (2nd ed.). Exeter, NH: Heinemann.

Clay, M.M. (1991). *Becoming literate: The construction of inner control.* Portsmouth, NH: Heinemann.

Clay, M.M. (1993). *Reading Recovery: A guidebook for teachers in training.* Portsmouth, NH: Heinemann.

Clay, M.M. (1998). *By different paths to common outcomes.* York, ME: Stenhouse.

Clay, M.M. (2000). *Running records for classroom teachers.* Portsmouth, NH: Heinemann.

Clay, M.M. (2002). *An observation survey of early literacy achievement* (2nd ed.). Portsmouth, NH: Heinemann.

Clay, M.M. (2005a). *Literacy lessons designed for individuals: Part one, why? when? and how?* Portsmouth, NH: Heinemann.

Clay, M.M. (2005b). *Literacy lessons designed for individuals: Part two, teaching procedures.* Portsmouth, NH: Heinemann.

Cunningham, J.W., Spadorcia, S.A., Erickson, K.A., Koppenhaver, D.A., Sturm, J.M., & Yoder, D.E. (2005). Investigating the instructional supportiveness of leveled texts. *Reading Research Quarterly, 40*(4), 410–427. doi:10.1598/RRQ.40.4.2

DeBacco, M. (2008, August 21). Guided reading...two words I have grown to hate [Web log]. Retrieved March 12, 2009, from marisadebacco.blogspot.com/2008/08/guided-readingtwo-words-i-have-grown-to.html

DeFord, D.E., Lyons, C.A., & Pinnell, G.S. (1991). *Bridges to literacy: Learning from Reading Recovery.* Portsmouth, NH: Heinemann.

Diller, D. (2007). *Making the most of small groups: Differentiation for all.* Portland, ME: Stenhouse.

DrivingPigeon. (2009, February 11). So, I hate guided reading [Web log]. Retrieved March 12, 2009, from forums.atozteacherstuff.com/showthread.php?t=79419

Duke, N.K., & Pearson, P.D. (2002). Effective practices for developing reading comprehension. In A.E. Farstrup & S.J. Samuels (Eds.), *What research has to say about reading instruction* (3rd ed., pp. 205–242). Newark, DE: International Reading Association.

Ford, M.P., & Opitz, M.F. (2008a). Guided reading: Then and now. In M.J. Fresch (Ed.), *An essential history of current reading practices* (pp. 66–81). Newark, DE: International Reading Association.

Ford, M.P., & Opitz, M.F. (2008b). A national survey of guided reading practices: What we can learn from primary teachers. *Literacy Research and Instruction, 47*(4), 309–331. doi:10.1080/19388070802332895

Fountas, I.C., & Pinnell, G.S. (1996). *Guided reading: Good first teaching for all children.* Portsmouth, NH: Heinemann.

Fountas, I.C., & Pinnell, G.S. (2005). *Leveled books, K–8: Matching texts to readers for effective teaching.* Portsmouth, NH: Heinemann.

Fountas, I.C., & Pinnell, G.S. (2006). *Teaching for comprehending and fluency: Thinking, talking, and writing about reading, K–8.* Portsmouth, NH: Heinemann.

Fountas, I.C., & Pinnell, G.S. (2007). *Fountas & Pinnell benchmark assessment system 2: Assessment guide.* Portsmouth, NH: Heinemann.

Gladwell, M. (2007). *Blink: The power of thinking without thinking.* New York: Back Bay.

Glynn, T. (1983). Building an effective teaching environment. In K. Wheldall & R.J. Riding (Eds.), *Psychological aspects of learning and teaching* (pp. 40–62). London: Croom Helm.

Goodman, K.S. (1985). A linguistic study of cues and miscues in reading. In H. Singer & R.B. Ruddell (Eds.), *Theoretical models and processes of reading* (3rd ed., pp. 129–134). Newark, DE: International Reading Association.

Gredler, M., & Shields, C. (2004). Does no one read Vygotsky's words? Commentary on Glassman. *Educational Researcher, 33*(2), 21–25. doi:10.3102/0013189X033002021

Gredler, M.E. (2007). Of cabbages and kings: Concepts and inferences curiously attributed to Lev Vygotsky (Commentary on McVee, Dunsmore, and Gavelek, 2005). *Review of Educational Research, 77*(2), 233–238. doi:10.3102/0034654306298270

Guastello, E.F., & Lenz, C.R. (2007). *The guided reading kidstation model: Making instruction meaningful for the whole class.* Newark, DE: International Reading Association.

Harvey, S., & Goudvis, A. (2007). *Strategies that work: Teaching comprehension for understanding and engagement* (2nd ed.). Portland, ME: Stenhouse.

Hill, S. (2001). Questioning text levels. *Australian Journal of Language and Literacy, 24*(1), 8–20.

Hoffman, J.V. (1998). When bad things happen to good ideas in literacy education: Professional dilemmas, personal decisions, and political traps. *The Reading Teacher, 52*(2), 102–112.

Holdaway, D. (1979). *The foundations of literacy.* New York: Ashton Scholastic.

Johnston, P.H. (2004). *Choice words: How our language affects children's learning.* Portland, ME: Stenhouse.

LaBerge, D., & Samuels, S.J. (1974). Toward a theory of automatic information processing in reading. *Cognitive Psychology, 6*(2), 293–323. doi:10.1016/0010-0285(74)90015-2

Mathewson, G.C. (2004). Model of attitude influence upon reading and learning to read. In R.B. Ruddell & N.J. Unrau (Eds.), *Theoretical models and processes of reading* (5th ed., pp. 1431–1461). Newark, DE: International Reading Association.

Miller, D. (2002). *Reading with meaning: Teaching comprehension in the primary grades.* Portland, ME: Stenhouse.

Mooney, M.E. (1990). *Reading to, with, and by children.* Katonah, NY: Richard C. Owen.

Opitz, M.F., & Ford, M.P. (2001). *Reaching readers: Flexible and innovative strategies for guided reading.* Portsmouth, NH: Heinemann.

Pearson, P.D., & Gallagher, M.C. (1983). The instruction of reading comprehension. *Contemporary Educational Psychology, 8*(3), 317–344. doi:10.1016/0361-476X(83)90019-X

Piaget, J. (1967). *Six psychological studies.* New York: Random House.

Pinnell, G.S., & Fountas, I.C. (2007). *The continuum of literacy learning, grades 3–8: A guide to teaching.* Portsmouth, NH: Heinemann.

Pinnell, G.S., & Fountas, I.C. (2009). *When readers struggle: Teaching that works.* Portsmouth, NH: Heinemann.

Pressley, M. (2000). What should comprehension instruction be the instruction of? In M.L. Kamil, P.B. Mosenthal, P.D. Pearson, & R. Barr (Eds.), *Handbook of reading research* (Vol. 3, pp. 545–561). Mahwah, NJ: Erlbaum.

Pressley, M., Johnson, C.J., Symons, S., McGoldrick, J.A., & Kurita, J.A. (1989). Strategies that improve children's memory and comprehension of text. *Elementary School Journal, 90*(1), 3–32. doi:10.1086/461599

Rasinski, T.V. (2003). *The fluent reader: Oral reading strategies for building word recognition, fluency, and comprehension.* New York: Scholastic.

Richardson, J. (2009). *The next step in guided reading: Focused assessments and targeted lessons for helping every student become a better reader.* New York: Scholastic.

Robb, L. (2000, May/June). The myth of learn to read/read to learn. *Instructor.* Retrieved September 5, 2009, from teacher.scholastic.com/professional/readexpert/mythread.htm

Rosenblatt, L.M. (2004). The transactional theory of reading and writing. In R.B. Ruddell & N.J. Unrau (Eds.), *Theoretical models and processes of reading* (5th ed., pp. 1363–1398). Newark, DE: International Reading Association.

Routman, R. (2003). *Reading essentials: The specifics you need to teach reading well.* Portsmouth, NH: Heinemann.

Ruddell, R.B., & Unrau, N.J. (2004). Reading as a meaning-construction process: The reader, the text, and the teacher. In R.B. Ruddell & N.J. Unrau (Eds.), *Theoretical models and processes of reading* (5th ed., pp. 1462–1521). Newark, DE: International Reading Association.

Spiro, R.J., Coulson, R.L., Feltovich, P.J., & Anderson, D.K. (2004). Cognitive flexibility theory: Advanced knowledge acquisition in ill-structured domains. In R.B. Ruddell & N.J. Unrau (Eds.), *Theoretical models and processes of reading* (5th ed., pp. 640–653). Newark, DE: International Reading Association.

Tharp, R.G., & Gallimore, R. (1988). *Rousing minds to life: Teaching, learning, and schooling in social context.* New York: Cambridge University Press.

Tyner, B. (2004). *Small-group reading instruction: A differentiated teaching model for beginning and struggling readers.* Newark, DE: International Reading Association.

Vygotsky, L.S. (1962). *Thought and language* (E. Hanfmann & G. Vakar, Eds. & Trans.). Cambridge, MA: MIT Press.

Watson, B. (1999). Creating independent learners. In J.S. Gaffney & B.J. Askew (Eds.), *Stirring the water: The influence of Marie Clay* (pp. 47–74). Portsmouth, NH: Heinemann.

White, B. (1993). *Mama makes up her mind: And other dangers of Southern living.* Reading, MA: Addison-Wesley.

Wood, D. (1994). *How children think and learn: An introduction to cognitive development.* Oxford, England: Basil Blackwell.

LITERATURE CITED

Bacon, R. (1997). *In my room.* Crystal Lake, IL: Rigby.

Cowley, J. (1990). *The ghost* (2nd ed.). Bothell, WA: Wright Group.

Greenfield, E. (1972). *Honey, I love and other love poems.* New York: HarperCollins.

Márquez, G.M. (2006). *One hundred years of solitude.* New York: HarperCollins.

Pearson, C.L. (1992). *Women I have known and been.* Placerville, CA: Gold Leaf.

White, E.B. (1999). *Charlotte's web.* New York: HarperCollins.

The world of Dick and Jane and friends. (2004). New York: Grosset & Dunlap.

INDEX

Note. Page numbers followed by *f* or *t* indicate figures or tables, respectively.

meaning: debate over reading instruction systems, 70; defined, 3; searching for, 78–80

Miller, D., xxii, 72, 84

mindful language, 65–67, 66*t*

"mining the book," 14

Modla, V.B., 73

Mooney, M.E., 15, 16

Moser, J., 27, 60

Mrs. Wishy Washy, 56

Murray, Donald, xxi

My Room (Bacon), 78, 79*f*

O

One Hundred Years of Solitude (Márquez), xxix, 53

Opitz, M.F., xiv, xviii, xx, xxii, 11, 53, 55

P

Paris, S.G., xxv

Pearson, C.L., 83

Pearson, P.D., xxv, xxvi, 11, 84

Piaget, J., xv, xxii, xxiii

Pinnell, G.S., xii, xiii, xvii–xviii, xxi, xxii, 13, 54, 56, 57, 72, 73, 75, 84–85, 88, 110

Pressley, M., 69, 84

print (visual cues): assessing integrating cues, 111–113; debate over reading instruction systems, 70, 80; defined, 3; as dimension of reading instruction, 3, 71; practicing reading as integrated process, 85–87, 86*t*; reading instruction and, 76–78; reading process for print-dependent readers, 5, 5*f*, 71, 111–112, 112*f*; relationship with story, 3–4, 4*f*; selecting texts based on, 45; as source of information, 3; tracking reading progress, 111, 112*f*; "uh-oh/you did it!" game, 94–95; understanding student reading processes, 104–107

problem-solving efforts: clarifying confusions from ineffective, 47–50, 50*t*; *Goldilocks and the Three Bears* example, 34–36; practicing reading as integrated process, 85–87, 86*t*; taking about thinking, 78–80

processing cues. *See* integrated processing

prompting when reading, 87–89, 88*t*

R

Rasinski, T.V., 16

read-alouds: about, 13–14; classroom scenario, 19–21; gradual release process and, 19, 19*t*

reading instruction: classroom scenario, 76–78; for comprehension, 73–76, 74*t*; connecting across contexts, 18–21; debates over, 70, 80; literacy story on, 82; for print, 76–78; print as dimension of, 3, 71; prompting during, 87–89, 88*t*; realigning, 69–70; reflection questions on, 81; for story, 76–78; story as dimension of, 3, 71–73; taking about thinking, 78–80

reading levels, instructional. *See* instructional reading levels

reading process. *See also* balanced reading process: assessing, 40*t*, 109–114, 112*f*, 114*t*; complexities of reading and, 1–2; difficulty with integration in, 6–8, 7*f*–8*f*; gradual release process stages and, 18, 19*t*; instructional contexts and, 13–18; literacy story on, 10; models for, 1, 8–9, 9*t*; relationship between print and story in, 4, 4*f*; selecting texts based on, 43–47; Student Placement Thought Sheet, 113, 119; vocabulary in, 2–8

Reading Recovery (Clay), 36

Reading Recovery model: adapting notations on running records, 107; controlled vocabulary and, 56; Croft and, xix, 40; guided reading and, xv–xvi; word recognition guidelines, 36

responsibility, gradual release of. *See* gradual release process

Richardson, J., xvii

Robb, L., 69

W

Watson, B., 89

White, B., 69

White, E.B., 31

Wood, D., xxiii

word recognition: Betts on, 32, 38;
breaking inefficient reading habits,
91, 91f; *Goldilocks and the Three Bears*
example, 34–36; instructional reading
levels and, 40–41; reading models on,
1, 8–9, 9t; Student Placement Thought
Sheet, 113, 119

The World of Dick and Jane: controlled
vocabulary and, 56–57, 62; story lines
in, 63–64

Y

You Can't Catch Me! (Hawes), 73